# THE
# APPLE·BARN
# COOKBOOK

**The Apple Barn and Cider Mill**
230 Apple Valley Road
Sevierville, Tennessee 37862

**The Apple Barn and Cider Mill**
230 Apple Valley Road
Sevierville, Tennessee 37862

800-421-4606
www.AppleBarnCiderMill.com

International Standard Book Number 0-9611508-2-3

WIMMER
COOKBOOKS

A CONSOLIDATED GRAPHICS COMPANY

800.548.2537   wimmerco.com

# TABLE OF CONTENTS

*Applewood* **FARMHOUSE** recipes appear after page 64

## HISTORY OF THE APPLE BARN

Between the business-like bustle of Sevierville and the tourist tempo of Pigeon Forge lies a lovely valley. Nature did its glorious part providing a spectacular view of the Smokies, a willow and sycamore lined path for the crystal clear Little Pigeon River, all in a natural amphitheater of gently rolling hills. Fittingly, the access to the valley is called Apple Valley Road.

For many years a small farmhouse stood by a shallow ford at the river's edge along what was then the main road between Sevierville and Gatlinburg. In 1921 the farmhouse burned and was replaced by a six-room farmhouse. The barn, built in the early 1900s, survived the fire.

### The Long Range Plan

With the goal of creating an ideal apple orchard, we, the Bon Hicks and Bill Kilpatrick families bought the 65-acre farm, farmhouse and barn from the owner at the time, Roger Mullendore. During the years we were studying apple growing, visiting other orchards and receiving help and advice from the county agent and extension service, we raised cattle and grew burley tobacco.

Then in the winter of 1976-1977, we felt we were ready to begin an orchard. That first year we planted 1100 trees of four different varieties: Golden Delicious, Red Delicious, Jonathan and Rome Beauty. Each year since then we have expanded the orchard until now we have whole hillsides covered with over 4200 trees and 14 varieties of apples: the original four plus Winesap, Empire, Paula Red, Cortland, Criterion, Arkansas Black, Ozark Gold, Jonagold, Prima and Mutsu.

### Saving the Old, Building the New

Part of the original purchase was an old cattle barn. Since it was of classic design our architect advised us to change its basic structure as little as possible. So we started our renovations with a thorough cleaning from top to bottom, one board at a time. Two of the stables were converted to a walk-in cooler for cider and apple storage. A concrete floor was added to a large shed on one side of the barn and a 150 gallon-per-hour cider press and refrigerated storage tanks were installed. Other stables and sheds were left untouched except for the addition of new floors of locally sawed white pine. What had been the hay feed rack was converted into long, attractive display counters for apples. Four stables were converted into separate display areas: one for jam, jelly, apple butter and molasses; one for dried fruits, nuts, popcorn and Indian corn; one for smoked country hams, bacon and Tennessee cheddar cheese and one for baskets and other local craft items.

### Open for Business

Then in the fall of 1981 the "Apple Barn and Cider Mill" opened for business. Its popularity has led to enlargements and improvements almost every year since. Customers wanted a pleasant place to sit and enjoy their cider, so in 1982 a cider bar was added with an outside deck extending into the orchard. The cider bar accommodates 60 people and its centerpiece is an antique soda fountain and back bar from the drugstore of Bill Kilpatrick's father. Around these priceless antiques, made from cherry, onyx and Tennessee pink marble, guests of the Apple Barn enjoy hot or cold fresh cider, apple donuts, apple dumplings, fresh baked apple and blueberry pie, applewood-smoked country ham on biscuits and our famous homemade fried apple pie.

### Additions, Additions, Additions.

In 1982 a smokehouse was added using hand-hewn pine and hand-split oak shakes to duplicate as closely as possible the smokehouses of the early settlers. Hams and bacon are also cured by the old time process, first treated with salt, pepper and sugar and then hung in the smokehouse for a long slow cure in a blend of the smoke from soldering applewood, hickory and corn cobs.

In 1986 we called on Huff & Ogle Enterprises of Gatlinburg to convert the old farmhouse into a full service country restaurant and to operate it. In 1987 the Applewood Farmhouse Restaurant opened and serves a wide variety of dishes for breakfast, lunch and dinner all "touched with the magic of apples." The restaurant has quickly become a favorite spot, not only for the excellent food and warm decor but also for beautiful views of the valley and the river, especially from the relaxing rocking chairs on the cool, breezy wrap-around porch.

Also in 1987 a candy factory was added to the Apple Barn and in the winter of 1987-1988 a major expansion of the Barn was completed carefully following the classic architectural lines which are so much a part of the heritage left by the early builders. The expansion permitted a larger pie kitchen and more room to make our apple butter.

## View from the Top

The top loft of the new bigger barn is an exciting place to visit. Looking up to the uncovered rafters gives you a wonderful feeling of ruggedly open space. From the top loft you can not only stand amid a big display of locally made baskets, you also have a commanding view of a maze of activities below. You can watch local craftsmen at work on the lower loft and see displays of their handiwork. From the second floor loft you can see down into the fascinating operation of the cider filling room, the beehive activities around the apple displays and the mail order area. And maybe the most exciting of all, your lofty vantage point is the ideal spot for "people watching" and makes you "lord of all you survey."

## Share Our Love of Apples

As you might expect, over the years since the Apple Barn was started we have had hundreds and hundreds of requests for our apple recipes and we have many of our friends and customers bring us their favorite apple recipes. So it seemed only a natural "labor of love" for Georgia, Nancy and the cooks in our organization to compile these recipes into a cookbook for all to enjoy. What a wonderful way to "have an apple a day and keep the you-know-who away."

Enjoy this collection of the apple goodies. And please come back to our storybook valley, the Apple Barn and Applewood Farmhouse Restaurant every time you are in the area. We promise both new discoveries and old-time treats and a real hospitable Smoky Mountain memory.

# CAKES

# THE APPLE BARN FRESH APPLE POUND CAKE
*Luscious apple all the way and easy to make.*

3 cups all-purpose flour, spooned into cup
1 teaspoon soda
1 teaspoon salt
1½ cups corn oil
2 cups sugar
3 large eggs, room temperature

2 teaspoons vanilla extract
1¼ cups pecans, medium-fine chopped
2 cups pared apples, finely chopped
Brown sugar topping (recipe follows)

Sift flour, soda and salt onto a platter or waxed paper. In a large bowl beat oil, sugar, eggs and vanilla at medium speed of electric mixer for 3 or 4 minutes until well blended. Gradually add flour mixture; beat until smooth. Fold in pecans and apples. Pour batter into a greased and floured bundt pan. Bake in a preheated 325 degrees oven about 1 hour 20 minutes, or until cake tests done. Cool on wire rack 20 minutes. For festive occasion, dribble brown sugar topping over warm cake. For an elegant dessert, slice cake and top each serving with baked custard. This cake is marvelous plain. Serve warm or cold. Store cake in foil or tin can for a day or two. To keep longer, refrigerate and bring to room temperature before serving. Fresh apples tend to mold easily.

Yield: one 10-inch bundt cake, 22 to 24 servings

**Brown Sugar Topping:**

½ cup butter or margarine
½ cup light brown sugar, firmly packed

2 teaspoons milk

Combine all ingredients and bring to a boil over medium heat; cook 2 minutes, stirring constantly. Spoon hot sugar mixture over warm cake.

*Georgia Kilpatrick*
*The Apple Barn*
*Sevierville, Tennessee*

# NANCY'S FRESH APPLE CAKE

1 cup vegetable oil
2 eggs
2 cups sugar
1½ cups all-purpose flour
1 teaspoon baking soda
1 teaspoon baking powder

1 teaspoon salt
1 teaspoon cinnamon
3 cups apples, peeled and
  chopped
1 cup pecans, chopped
1 cup butterscotch morsels

Beat together oil, eggs and sugar. Sift together next 5 ingredients. Add sifted dry ingredients alternately with apples to egg mixture; mix well. Stir in pecans and half of morsels. Spread batter in a greased 9x13-inch baking pan. Sprinkle with remaining morsels. Bake at 350 degrees for 1 hour. Serve in small portions as this is a very rich cake.

*Nancy Hicks*
*The Apple Barn*
*Sevierville, Tennessee*


# TOPSY-TURVY APPLE COFFEE CAKE

¾ cup butter or margarine,
  divided
⅓ cup brown sugar
1 teaspoon cinnamon
¼ cup pecans, chopped
2 cups sliced apples

½ teaspoon baking soda
1 cup sour cream
2 eggs
1½ cups all-purpose flour
1 cup sugar
1½ teaspoons baking powder

Melt ¼ cup butter in 8-inch square baking dish; blend in brown sugar and cinnamon. Sprinkle pecans over brown sugar; place apple slices in single layer over nuts. Stir baking soda into sour cream and allow to stand 10 minutes. Cream remaining ½ cup butter; add eggs and beat thoroughly. Stir flour, sugar and baking powder together. Add dry ingredients and sour cream alternately to creamed mixture, beginning and ending with dry ingredients. Pour over apples; bake at 350 degrees for 45 to 50 minutes or until toothpick inserted in center comes out clean. Cool in dish 10 minutes; invert onto serving dish.

Yield: 1 single layer cake.

# OLD FASHIONED STACK CAKE

2 cups sugar
1 cup butter or shortening
2 eggs
6 cups sifted all-purpose flour
1 teaspoon soda

3 teaspoons baking powder
1 teaspoon salt
1 teaspoon vanilla
½ cup buttermilk

Cream sugar and butter or shortening together. Add eggs 1 at a time beating well after each addition. Sift flour, soda, baking powder and salt together. Add alternately to batter with buttermilk; add vanilla. Chill dough for 3 or 4 hours. Divide dough into 6 or 7 parts. Use well floured board, on which to roll out layers. Bake on cookie sheet until slightly browned at 450 degrees for 10 to 15 minutes. Spread each layer with dried apple filling. Do not spread filling on top layer. Let stand in a covered container at least 12 hours before cutting.

**Apple Filling:**

1 pound dried apples
1 cup brown sugar
1 cup white sugar

2 teaspoons cinnamon
½ teaspoon allspice

Wash apples; cover with water and cook until tender. Mash thoroughly; add sugars and spices. Cool before spreading between layers.

*Louise Kilpatrick*
*Vonore, Tennessee*

# APPLE FRUIT CAKE

½ cup butter
1 cup light brown sugar, firmly
  packed
1 egg
1 teaspoon vanilla
1¾ cups all-purpose flour
1 teaspoon baking powder
½ teaspoon baking soda
½ teaspoon cinnamon

½ teaspoon nutmeg
½ teaspoon salt
¼ cup milk
1½ cups Golden Delicious
  Apples, cored, pared, and
  finely chopped
1 cup raisins or chopped dates
1 cup mixed candied fruit
1 cup nuts, chopped

In mixing bowl, cream butter; gradually add sugar and beat until light and fluffy. Beat in egg and vanilla. Sift together flour, baking powder, soda, cinnamon, nutmeg and salt; add to creamed mixture alternately with milk, beginning and ending with dry ingredients. Fold in apples, raisins, mixed fruits and nuts. Spread evenly in a 9x5x3-inch loafpan lined with waxed paper. Bake 2½ to 3 hours in preheated 275 degrees oven. Cool in pan. Remove paper; wrap and store in cool place.

Yield: 1 cake

# FRESH APPLE-DATE CAKE

2 cups sugar
1½ cups vegetable oil
3 eggs
3 cups all-purpose flour
1 teaspoon soda
1 teaspoon baking powder
1 teaspoon salt

1 teaspoon ground cinnamon
1 teaspoon ground nutmeg
2 teaspoons vanilla
3 cups firm apples, chopped
1 cup pitted dates, chopped
1 cup pecans, chopped

Combine sugar and vegetable oil in large bowl. Stir to mix well. Add eggs, one at a time; beating well after each addition. Combine dry ingredients and stir into the oil mixture. Add vanilla, chopped apples, dates and pecans; mix well. Spoon batter into greased 10-inch tube pan and bake at 325 degrees for 1½ hours, or until cake tests done.

Yield: one 10-inch tube cake

# SUGAR 'N SPICE APPLE CAKES

2 cups all-purpose flour
1 cup whole wheat flour
1½ cups sugar, divided
4 teaspoons baking powder
1 teaspoon salt
1 teaspoon nutmeg
⅔ cup shortening

½ cup milk
2 eggs, beaten
2 cups finely chopped apples
½ cup butter or margarine, melted
1½ teaspoons cinnamon

Combine flours, 1 cup sugar, baking powder, salt and nutmeg. Cut in shortening until mixture resembles fine crumbs. Combine milk and eggs; gradually add to dry ingredients. Fold in apples. Fill greased muffin tins ⅔ full with batter. Bake at 350 degrees for 20 to 25 minutes. Combine remaining ½ cup sugar and cinnamon. While cakes are warm, dip tops in melted butter, then in cinnamon sugar. Best when served warm.

Yield: 18 cakes

# BIG APPLE CAKE

1½ cups oil
2 cups sugar
3 eggs
3 cups all-purpose flour
1 teaspoon soda

2 teaspoons cinnamon
½ teaspoon mace
½ teaspoon salt
3 cups apples, chopped
2 teaspoons vanilla

Mix oil and sugar; add eggs one at a time. Sift dry ingredients and add to mixture. Fold in apples and vanilla. Pour into greased 10-inch tube pan. Bake at 325 degrees for 1¼ hours.

Yield: 10 to 12 servings

# APPLE CHEESECAKE ELEGANTE

1 (10½-ounce) package cheesecake mix
¼ cup sugar
¼ cup butter or margarine, melted
⅓ cup ground or finely chopped walnuts
1½ cups cold milk
2 cups canned applesauce
½ teaspoon grated lemon rind
2 tablespoons lemon juice
¼ cup brown sugar
2 tablespoons butter or margarine
½ teaspoon cinnamon
½ teaspoon nutmeg
¼ teaspoon mace

## CRUST:
To make crust empty envelope of graham cracker crust from cheesecake mix into a bowl. Add ¼ cup sugar, ¼ cup melted butter or margarine and nuts. Mix until thoroughly combined. Press mixture firmly against sides and bottom of an 8-inch pieplate. Refrigerate 5 minutes or bake in 375 degree oven for 8 minutes. Cool.

## FILLING:
Pour milk into a small mixing bowl. Add contents of cheesecake filling envelope from cheesecake, mix ½ cup applesauce, and grated lemon rind. Beat at low speed with electric mixer or rotary beater until blended. Beat at medium speed 3 minutes longer. Pour into prepared crust; chill at least 1 hour.

## TOPPING:
Combine 1½ cups applesauce and remaining ingredients in saucepan; simmer for 20 minutes. To serve, top wedges of cake with spiced applesauce topping. Topping may be served warm or cold.

Yield: 6 to 8 servings

# FRESH APPLE CAKE

2 cups sugar
1½ cups oil
3 eggs, beaten
3 cups all-purpose flour
1 teaspoon salt

1 teaspoon soda
2 teaspoons vanilla
3 cups eating apples, chopped
1 cup pecans, chopped

Mix together sugar, oil and eggs. Sift together dry ingredients. Blend together in order given. Bake at 350 degrees in greased tube pan for 1 hour 15 minutes. Batter will be stiff.

## TOPPING:

⅓ cup margarine
¼ cup evaporated milk

1 cup brown sugar

Melt together in saucepan. Boil for 3 minutes. Add 1 teaspoon vanilla. Spread over warm cake.

# ROSY APPLE DREAM

⅓ cup margarine, softened
1 cup all-purpose flour
1 tablespoon sugar
¾ teaspoon baking powder
¼ teaspoon salt
1 egg
1 tablespoon milk

6 cups apples, peeled and sliced
1 (3-ounce) package strawberry
   gelatin
2 tablespoons sugar
1 cup flour
1 cup sugar
½ cup margarine

Combine first 7 ingredients in small mixing bowl; beat until smooth. Spread in bottom of greased springform pan. Pile apples on crust and shake pan to settle slices. Combine gelatin with 2 tablespoons sugar; sprinkle over apples. Combine flour and sugar; cut in margarine until crumbly. Sprinkle over all. Bake at 350 degrees for 1 hour. Chill thoroughly.

Yield: 12 to 16 servings

# APPLE-RAISIN RUM CAKE

½ cup butter
1 cup white sugar
½ cup brown sugar
2 eggs
2 cups all-purpose flour
1½ teaspoons baking powder
1 teaspoon salt
½ teaspoon baking soda

1 teaspoon cinnamon
½ teaspoon nutmeg
1 cup evaporated milk
2 tablespoons rum
2 cups apples, chopped
2 cups raisins
Chopped nuts (optional)

In a bowl cream the butter, then beat in the sugars until light and fluffy. Beat in eggs; sift together flour, baking powder, salt, soda, cinnamon and nutmeg. Add dry ingredients alternately with the undiluted evaporated milk and rum to creamed mixture. Mix in chopped apples, raisins and nuts. Pour into a greased 9x12x12-inch pan. Bake in a 350 degrees oven for about 40 minutes or until cake springs back when touched.

Yield: one 9x12x12 cake

# RAW APPLE CAKE

2 cups sugar
1½ cups cooking oil
3 eggs
3 cups all-purpose flour
1 teaspoon ground cinnamon
1 teaspoon salt

1 teaspoon soda
1 teaspoon vanilla
2 cups flaked coconut
3 cups diced, tart, raw apples
1 cup chopped pecans

Cream together sugar and cooking oil. Add eggs and beat well. Combine flour, cinnamon, salt and soda; gradually add to egg mixture. Add vanilla, coconut, apples and nuts. Batter will be thick. Pour batter into a greased and floured tube pan. Bake at 325 degrees for 1½ to 2 hours or until done. VARIATION: May add 1 cup chopped dates if desired.

# APPLESAUCE CAKE

½ cup shortening
1 cup sugar
1½ cups applesauce
1 cup raisins
2 cups sifted all-purpose flour
1 teaspoon cinnamon

1 teaspoon nutmeg
2 teaspoons soda
½ teaspoon cloves
½ teaspoon salt
½ cup nut pieces

Cream shortening and sugar. Heat applesauce; add with raisins to sugar mixture. Cool. Sift dry ingredients together, and gradually beat into sugar mixture. Add nuts. Pour into greased 9x5x3-inch loafpan. Bake in 325 degrees oven, 1 hour. Turn out on rack to cool.

Yield: 1 loafpan cake

# APPLE-RAISIN COFFEE CAKE

¾ cup sugar
¼ cup shortening
1 egg
½ cup milk
1½ cups all-purpose flour
2 teaspoons baking powder

½ teaspoon salt
½ cup seedless raisins
1 cup apples, peeled and sliced
1 teaspoon cinnamon
2 tablespoons sugar

Beat ¾ cup sugar, shortening and egg until creamy; stir in milk. Sift flour, baking powder and salt together. Add raisins to flour mixture and stir into creamed mixture. Spread batter in greased and floured 9x9-inch pan. Arrange apple slices on top of batter, pressing in slightly. Mix cinnamon and 2 tablespoons sugar; sprinkle over apple slices. Bake in 375 degrees oven 35 minutes. Serve warm.

Yield: 9 servings

# APPLE CHIP PUDDING CAKE

2 cups sugar
1¼ cups vegetable oil
2 eggs, beaten
1½ cups all-purpose flour
1 teaspoon soda
1 teaspoon salt
1 teaspoon cinnamon

1 teaspoon vanilla
3 cups apples, peeled and
    chopped
¾ cup dates, chopped
½ cup walnuts, chopped
½ cup golden raisins

In mixer bowl beat together sugar, oil and eggs. Sift together flour, soda, salt and cinnamon. Reserve small portion of dry mixture to coat fruit and nuts. Add flour mixture to beaten sugar mixture and blend well; stir in vanilla and apples. Dredge with reserved flour mixture, dates, walnuts and raisins; stir. Pour into 1 large 13x9-inch pan, or 2 smaller pans. Bake at 350 degrees in metal pan or 325 degrees in glass pan for about 45 minutes.

*Sherry Lemasters*
*Sevierville, Tennessee*

# FRESH APPLE COFFEE CAKE

1 cup sugar
½ cup shortening
1 egg
1½ cups all-purpose flour
1 teaspoon soda
1 teaspoon salt

2 cups apples, peeled and
    chopped
2 tablespoons all-purpose flour
⅓ cup brown sugar, packed
1 teaspoon ground cinnamon
½ cup pecans, chopped

Cream sugar and shortening until light and fluffy; add egg, and beat well. Combine 1½ cups flour, soda and salt; add to creamed mixture, mixing well. Combine apples with 2 tablespoons flour; stir into batter. Pour batter into a greased 10x6x2-inch baking dish. Combine brown sugar, cinnamon and pecans; sprinkle over batter. Bake at 350 degrees for 40 minutes.

Yield: 8 servings

# APPLE CRUNCH CAKE

2 cups flour
1½ teaspoons salt
1 teaspoon nutmeg
1 teaspoon cinnamon
1 teaspoon soda
1¼ cups oil

2 eggs
2 cups sugar
2 cups fresh apples, sliced
1 cup chopped nuts
1 teaspoon vanilla
⅓ cup brandy

Sift together flour, salt, nutmeg, cinnamon and soda. Mix oil, eggs and sugar. Add flour mixture to oil mixture and mix well. Add apples, nuts, vanilla and brandy; mix again. Batter will be very stiff like a cookie dough. Spread into lightly greased 13x5x2-inch pan. Bake at 350 degrees for 35 to 45 minutes. This is a very rich cake and should not be iced. The crust is crunchy like a cookie and the inside is moist and chewy like a brownie.

# APPLE-SCOTCH LOAF CAKE

1½ cups sugar
3 eggs
½ cup oil
1 teaspoon vanilla
2½ cups all-purpose flour
2 teaspoons baking powder
1 teaspoon soda

1 teaspoon cinnamon
1 teaspoon salt
4 cups apples, diced and
  unpeeled
1 cup nuts, chopped (optional)
1 cup butterscotch chips

Mix sugar, eggs, oil and vanilla. Add flour mixed with baking powder, soda, cinnamon and salt; mix well. Stir in nuts and apples. Spread in well greased 9x13-inch pan. Sprinkle top with butterscotch chips and bake at 350 degrees for 30 to 40 minutes, or until done.

# STACK CAKE

**1 lb. dried apples**

Soak apples a few hours or overnight. Cook until tender. Run through colander; sweeten and spice to taste.

**Stack Cake Dough:**

| | |
|---|---|
| 6 cups self-rising flour | 2 eggs |
| 1 cup milk | 2 tablespoons vanilla (optional) |
| 1½ cups white sugar | ⅔ cup vegetable shortening |

Mix enough flour to make a real stiff dough. Makes about 8 layers. Roll dough out on waxed paper. Cut with fluted or regular piepan. Lift dough with waxed paper and place on cookie sheet to bake. Bake at 350 degrees until nice and brown. Have apples hot. Place a layer of cake on plate and cover with apples. Repeat until stacked.

*Lennie Kent*
*Cosby, Tennessee*

# ROBIN'S FRUIT DESSERT

| | |
|---|---|
| 5 cups apples, thinly sliced | 5⅓ tablespoons butter, melted |
| 8 ounces of white cake mix | 1 cup rich milk |

Butter your baking dish or pan heavily. Spread fresh fruit in bottom of pan. Most cake mixes are one pound—use ½ the box. Spread mix over the fresh apples. Dot the dry mix generously with butter. Pour rich milk or cream over all. Bake at 350 degrees for about 30 minutes or until nicely browned. Serve warm with milk or whipped cream.

# APPLE CINNAMON COFFEE CAKE

1 cup butter or margarine
1¼ cups sugar
2 eggs
1 cup sour cream
1 teaspoon vanilla
2 cups all-purpose flour
1 teaspoon baking powder

½ teaspoon soda
1 cup apples, peeled and finely
  chopped
1 cup pecans, chopped
1 teaspoon cinnamon
¼ cup sugar

Cream butter and sugar until light and fluffy; add eggs, sour cream and vanilla, beating well. Sift together flour, baking powder and soda; beat into butter mixture. Stir in finely chopped apples and pecans. In another bowl, combine cinnamon and sugar. Spread ½ of apple batter in a well-greased and floured tube pan. Sprinkle ½ of cinnamon and sugar mixture over batter. Distribute remaining batter evenly on top, and sprinkle with remaining sugar and cinnamon. Bake in preheated 350 degrees oven for 60 to 70 minutes, or until lightly browned, and a toothpick inserted in center comes out clean. Remove to a cooling rack for 20 minutes before taking cake from pan. Dust lightly with powdered sugar, and serve either warm or cool.

Yield: 1 coffee cake

# COOKIES
# AND
# PIES

# GLAZED APPLE GEMS

½ cup butter or margarine
1⅓ cups brown sugar, packed
1 egg
1 large apple, peeled, cored and
  finely chopped
1 cup raisins
1 cup nuts, finely chopped

¼ cup apple juice
1 teaspoon grated lemon peel
3 cups all-purpose flour
1 teaspoon baking soda
1 teaspoon cinnamon
1 teaspoon nutmeg

Glaze:

1½ cups sifted powdered sugar
3 tablespoons apple or lemon
  juice

1 tablespoon butter

Cream butter with sugar in large bowl until light and fluffy. Stir in egg, apples, raisins, nuts, apple juice and lemon peel. Blend in flour, baking soda, cinnamon and nutmeg and mix well. Drop dough by teaspoons on greased cookie sheet and bake at 375 degrees for 10 to 12 minutes. Prepare glaze by mixing ingredients in food processor or blender. Transfer to bowl. Remove cookies from oven. Let cool slightly on wire rack. Dip top of each warm cookie into glaze swirling to cover. Return to rack and cool completely. Store in airtight container.

# SPICED APPLE BARS

½ cup shortening
1 cup sugar
1 egg
1 teaspoon vanilla
2 cups all-purpose flour
2 teaspoons baking powder
1 teaspoon cinnamon

½ teaspoon nutmeg
2 tablespoons cocoa
½ teaspoon soda (dissolved in
  milk)
⅔ cup milk
1½ cups apples, diced

Cream shortening and sugar; beat in egg and vanilla. Add dry ingredients alternately with milk. Stir in apples. Bake in greased, floured 13x9-inch pan at 350 degrees for 25 minutes.

# SOFT MOLASSES APPLE COOKIES

½ cup shortening
½ cup sugar
1 egg
1 cup molasses
1 tablespoon lemon juice
3½ cups sifted all-purpose flour
1 teaspoon cinnamon

¾ teaspoon ground cloves
½ teaspoon ginger
2 teaspoons baking soda
⅛ teaspoon salt
⅓ cup boiling water
1 cup tart apples, pared,
    cored and finely chopped

Cream shortening and sugar. Beat in egg. Stir in molasses and lemon juice; blend well. Sift together dry ingredients; add to creamed mixture. Stir in boiling water; mix well. Add chopped apples; mix. Chill thoroughly. Drop by teaspoons on greased baking sheets. Bake in 350 degrees oven for 8 to 10 minutes.

Yield: 5 dozen

# APPLE BROWNIES

⅔ cup soft margarine
1¾ cups brown sugar
2 eggs
1 teaspoon vanilla
2 cups flour
2 teaspoons baking powder

¼ teaspoon salt
⅓ cup chopped walnuts
1 cup chopped, peeled apples
⅓ cup raisins
Powdered sugar

Cream margarine and brown sugar. Add eggs and beat until well mixed. Add vanilla and mix again. Add sifted dry ingredients and beat until mixture is smooth. Add apples, walnuts and raisins and stir gently with a strong spoon. Spread batter in a greased 9x13-inch pan and bake at 350 degrees for 30 to 35 minutes. Remove brownies from pan and roll each one in sifted powdered sugar.

Yield: 1½ dozen

# PEANUT BUTTER-APPLE TEA STICKS

1 egg
¾ cup brown sugar, packed
½ cup peanut butter
¼ cup milk
1 teaspoon vanilla
Sifted powdered sugar

¾ cup sifted all-purpose flour
1 teaspoon baking powder
½ teaspoon ground cinnamon
¼ teaspoon salt
1 cup chopped, peeled apples

Preheat oven to 350 degrees. Beat egg until light. Beat in brown sugar, add peanut butter, milk and vanilla; mix well. Stir together flour, baking powder, cinnamon and salt; stir into peanut butter mixture. Stir in apples. Bake in 350 degrees oven for 30 to 35 minutes. Cool for 5 minutes. Cut into rectangles. Roll in powdered sugar.

Yield: 2 dozen

# APPLESAUCE COOKIES

1 cup sugar
½ cup shortening
1 egg
1½ cups unsweetened applesauce
2 teaspoons soda
2¼ cups all-purpose flour

½ teaspoon ground cloves
1 teaspoon cinnamon
½ teaspoon salt
1 cup raisins
½ cup nuts

Cream together sugar, shortening and eggs. Add applesauce in which soda has been dissolved. Sift in flour, spices and salt; add raisins and nuts. Drop several inches apart onto greased baking sheet. Bake at 300 degrees about 15 minutes.

Yield: 30 cookies

# FRIED APPLE PIES

4 large tart apples, peeled,
  cored and sliced
3 tablespoons water
¾ cup sugar
½ teaspoon cinnamon

3 cups flour
1½ teaspoons salt
1 cup shortening
6 to 8 tablespoons ice water
Cooking oil

In a 2-quart pan, cook apples with water over medium heat until apples reach the consistency of applesauce. Add sugar and cinnamon and continue cooking 5 minutes longer; stirring often. Remove from heat and cool. While apples are cooking, prepare pastry. Sift together the flour and salt. With two knives or a pastry blender, cut ½ cup shortening into flour until shortening is pea-sized, evenly distributed throughout. Cut in remaining ½ cup shortening until shortening is about the size of navy beans. Gradually add ice water just until mixture forms a ball. Wrap in waxed paper and refrigerate 20 minutes. On a lightly floured board, roll out pastry 1/16-inch thick. Cut circles, 6-inches in diameter, out of pastry, rerolling and cutting all scraps until all pastry is used. Brush edges with ice water and place 2 tablespoons cooled apple filling on ½ of each pastry. Fold pastry in ½ and crimp edges with a fork. Prick fork tines into top side of pies to allow steam to escape. Cover the bottom of a frying pan with almost ¼-inch of oil and heat thoroughly. When a small scrap of pastry sizzles when placed in the oil; pan is ready. Carefully place pies in frying pan, two at a time, and brown evenly on 1 side before turning once to brown the other side. Remove from pan and dust with powdered sugar as desired.

Yield: 1 dozen

# APPLE MERINGUE PIE

1 (9-inch) baked pastry shell          ½ cup raisins
6 cups tart apples, pared and
  cored

Cook apples and raisins with ¾ cup water for 15 minutes at medium heat until apples are tender. Remove from heat; drain excess liquid.

Gently fold in:
1 cup sugar                           3 egg yolks, well beaten
1 tablespoon butter                   Rind and juice from 1 lemon
2 tablespoons flour

Return to heat. Cook for 5 minutes or until thickened. Spoon into baked pastry shell. Spread meringue over filling, sealing to edge of pastry. Bake at 350 degrees, or until meringue is golden.

Meringue:

3 egg whites                          ½ teaspoon vanilla
¼ teaspoon cream of tartar            6 tablespoons sugar

Beat egg whites with cream of tartar and vanilla until soft peaks form. Gradually add sugar and beat until stiff.

Yield: one 9-inch pie

# GOLDEN APPLE TORTE

2 cups all-purpose flour
½ cup sugar
2 teaspoons baking powder
Dash salt
½ cup soft butter or margarine
1 egg
2 tablespoons cold water

5 medium Golden Delicious
  apples
Juice of ½ lemon
¼ cup raisins
⅓ cup sugar
2 tablespoons flour
1 teaspoon cinnamon

Sift together 2 cups flour, ½ cup sugar, baking powder and salt. With fingers blend in butter or margarine, egg and water until dough holds together. Chill ⅓ of dough. Pat remaining ⅔ of dough on bottom and half way up sides of greased 9-inch springform pan. Bake at 400 degrees for 10 minutes. Peel, core and slice apples. Toss with lemon juice and raisins. Mix ⅓ cup sugar with 2 tablespoons flour and cinnamon; toss with apples. Turn into prepared crust. Roll out chilled dough and cut into ½-inch strips. Arrange in lattice over apples, sealing to edges of baked pastry. Bake at 350 degrees for 50 to 60 minutes, until apples are tender and crust is golden brown.

Yield: 8 to 10 servings

# APPLE CRUMB PIE

3 large cooking apples,
  peeled, cored and thinly sliced
1 unbaked 9-inch pastry shell
1 teaspoon ground cinnamon

1 cup sugar, divided
¾ cup all-purpose flour
⅓ cup margarine

Arrange apple slices evenly in pastry shell. Combine cinnamon and ½ cup sugar; stir well, and sprinkle mixture over apples. Combine flour and remaining sugar; stir well. Cut margarine into flour mixture with a pastry blender until mixture resembles course meal. Sprinkle over apples. Bake at 400 degrees for 40 to 50 minutes.

Yield: one 9-inch pie

*Nancy Hicks*
*The Apple Barn*
*Sevierville, Tennessee*

# APPLE PECAN CRUMB PIE

¼ cup pecans, chopped
1 (9-inch) deep, unbaked, pie shell
6 cups apples, peeled and
  sliced
1 cup sugar

2 teaspoons flour
¼ teaspoon nutmeg
½ teaspoon cinnamon
2 tablespoons margarine

Sprinkle pecans in pie shell. Mix sugar, flour and spices; toss with apples. Heap apples in pie shell; dot with margarine.

**Crumb Topping:**

½ cup brown sugar, packed
¼ cup margarine
⅓ cup flour

¼ teaspoon cinnamon
¼ cup pecans, chopped

Blend crumb topping ingredients with fork until size of peas; sprinkle over pie. Bake at 425 degrees for 40 to 45 minutes.

# HARVEST TABLE APPLE PIE

6 medium apples, sliced
1 tablespoon cornstarch
1 teaspoon cinnamon
¼ teaspoon salt

3 tablespoons sugar
3 tablespoons melted margarine
⅓ cup white syrup

Prepare pastry for a two-crust 9-inch pie. Fill bottom shell with 6 medium apples, sliced. Combine remaining ingredients and pour over apples. Cover with top crust and bake in 425 degrees oven 45 minutes, or until crust is browned.

**Topping:**

¼ cup brown sugar
2 tablespoons flour
3 tablespoons white syrup

2 tablespoons margarine,
  softened
¼ cup chopped nuts

Mix ingredients together, spread over top of pie. Return to oven for 10 minutes or until topping is bubbly. (Place pie pan on larger pan to catch topping that may run off).

Yield: One 9-inch pie

# CHEESE CRUMBLE APPLE PIE

**Crumble Topping:**
1 (9¼-ounce) package pie crust
  mix, divided
½ cup granulated sugar
½ cup brown sugar, firmly
  packed
¾ teaspoon ground cinnamon
3 tablespoons butter or
  margarine

**Filling:**
2 cups shredded Cheddar
  cheese, divided
2 to 2½ tablespoons water
6 cups cooking apples, peeled
  and sliced
1 tablespoon flour
¼ teaspoon grated nutmeg

For topping, divide pie crust mixture in half. Mix ½ with sugars and cinnamon, cut in butter thoroughly; set aside. Use other ½ for bottom crust of pie. Combine 1 cup shredded cheese with remaining pie crust. Stir in 2 to 2½ tablespoons water, mix well, and roll dough to fit a 9-inch pieplate. Place apples in pastry-lined plate; sprinkle flour over apples. Dust with nutmeg, and cover with ½ the crumble topping. Spread remaining 1 cup shredded cheese over mixture, and top with remaining crumble topping. Bake at 375 degrees about 40 minutes, or until apples are tender.

Yield: one 9-inch pie

# APPLE-SOUR CREAM PIE

Pastry for 9-inch lattice-top pie
1 egg, beaten
⅔ cup granulated sugar
⅓ cup brown sugar

1 cup dairy sour cream
4 cups tart apples, cored, pared,
  and thinly sliced
½ cup light raisins

Line a 9-inch pieplate with pastry. Combine egg, sugars and sour cream; stir in sliced apples and raisins. Turn into pastry shell. Add lattice top; seal edges and flute. Bake in 400 degrees oven for 50 minutes or until done, covering edges with foil during last 15 minutes baking time.

Yield: one 9-inch pie

# CRISP CRUST APPLE PIE

Filling:

5 medium apples (Red or Golden
  Delicious)
1½ cups sugar
1 tablespoon flour

1 teaspoon cinnamon (more or
  less depending on taste)
½ cup water

Slice apples thin into an oblong baking dish. Mix together sugar, flour and cinnamon, sprinkle over apples. Pour water over mixture.

Crust:

2½ cups self-rising flour
½ teaspoon salt
⅔ cup shortening
About ½ cup ice water

¾ cup sugar
1 teaspoon cinnamon
½ cup butter or margarine

Mix flour and salt; cut in shortening. Add enough water to hold dough together. Roll between sheets of waxed paper. Put on top of apple mixture. Sprinkle on sugar and cinnamon (mixed together). Dot with butter cut into patties. Bake at 400 degrees until crust is browned and apples are tender. (When I have been in a rush, I have used 2 frozen pie shells for crust and put on topping).

*Pat Kent*
*Cosby, Tennessee*

# GRATED APPLE PIE

4 large apples
1 cup sugar
½ teaspoon ground cinnamon
Pastry for double-crust 9-inch pie

2 tablespoons butter or
  margarine
¼ cup sugar, if desired

Wash apples and grate (do not peel). Add 1 cup sugar and the cinnamon; mix well. Spoon mixture into pastry-lined 9-inch piepan. Cover top with lattice strips. Dot with butter and sprinkle with ¼ cup sugar, if desired. Bake at 350 degrees for 1 hour or until browned.

Yield: one 9-inch pie

# CRUMB-TOP BROWN SUGAR APPLE PIE

5 cups apples, peeled and sliced
¾ cup brown sugar, packed
2 tablespoons flour
⅛ teaspoon salt
1½ teaspoons cinnamon
¼ teaspoon nutmeg
¼ teaspoon mace
1 (9-inch) pie shell, unbaked

Crumb Topping:
2 tablespoons brown sugar
2 tablespoons sugar
⅛ teaspoon nutmeg
⅛ teaspoon cinnamon
⅛ teaspoon salt
3 tablespoons flour
2 tablespoons margarine

Combine first 7 ingredients; toss to mix thoroughly. Heap in pie shell. Combine topping ingredients and mix until crumbly; sprinkle over pie. Bake at 425 degrees for 45 minutes. Allow to cool 30 minutes before serving.

# WHOLE WHEAT APPLE PIE

¾ cup unsifted white flour
¾ cup unsifted whole wheat flour
½ teaspoon salt
½ cup margarine
5 or 6 tablespoons ice water

¾ cup sugar
1 tablespoon tapioca
¼ teaspoon ground cinnamon
6 cups apples, sliced and peeled
2 tablespoons margarine

Combine flours and salt in bowl. Cut in ½ cup margarine with a pastry blender or two knives until mixture resembles coarse meal. Stir in ice water; mix lightly. Form dough into a ball. On a lightly floured board, roll out ½ dough to fit a 9-inch pie plate. Transfer to plate and trim edge leaving ½-inch overhanging. Combine sugar, tapioca and cinnamon. Mix with apples. Pile into pie plate. Dot top with 2 tablespoons margarine. Roll out remaining pastry and cut 2-inch slits in center. Cover pie; seal edges and flute. Bake at 400 degrees 45 to 50 minutes, or until done.

**Wheat Germ Apple Pie:** Prepare pastry as above adding 2 tablespoons wheat germ to the flour and salt mixture. Also, add 2 tablespoons wheat germ to the filling.

Yield: one 9-inch pie

# CARAMEL-TOPPED APPLE PIE

5½ cups apples, peeled and
    sliced
¼ cup water
¾ cup granulated sugar
1 tablespoon flour
½ teaspoon ground cinnamon
½ teaspoon ground nutmeg

½ cup chopped pecans
¾ cup graham cracker crumbs
¼ teaspoon salt
⅓ cup melted butter or
    margarine
½ pound caramels
½ cup hot milk

Combine apples and water in saucepan. Cover and steam about 3
minutes. Drain and spread apples on cookie sheet to cool quickly. Arrange slices in 9- or 10-inch pieplate. Combine sugar, flour, cinnamon,
nutmeg, pecans, graham cracker crumbs, salt, and melted butter or
margarine; sprinkle over apples. Bake at 425 degrees for 10 minutes
then reduce heat to 350 degrees and bake for 20 minutes. While pie is
baking, combine caramels and hot milk in top of a double boiler; cook
until caramels are melted. Pour the hot caramel sauce over top of pie
and continue baking for an additional 10 minutes. Cool before serving.

Yield: one 9- or 10-inch pie

# NO-CRUST APPLE PIE

¾ cup sugar
½ cup all-purpose flour
1 egg
¼ teaspoon cinnamon
¼ teaspoon nutmeg

1 teaspoon baking powder
½ teaspoon vanilla
¼ teaspoon salt
½ cup nuts, chopped
1 cup apples, peeled and chopped

Mix sugar, flour and egg. Add next 5 ingredients; blend well. Stir in nuts
and apples. Pour into greased 9-inch piepan. Bake at 350 degrees for 30
minutes. Allow to cool 10 minutes before serving.

# HONEY APPLE PIE

1 (9-inch) unbaked pie shell
1 cup sugar
3 tablespoons flour
¼ cup honey
⅓ cup heavy cream

5 tart apples, peeled, cored, and
   cut in thin slices
½ teaspoon ground cinnamon
¼ teaspoon ground nutmeg
1 tablespoon butter or margarine

Sprinkle pastry with 1 tablespoon each of sugar and flour. Combine the remaining sugar and flour; stir in honey and cream. Pour this mixture over apples in large bowl. Mix gently until slices are well coated. Spoon apples into pie shell and dust with cinnamon and nutmeg; dot with butter. Bake at 375 degrees for 35 to 40 minutes.

Yield: one 9-inch pie

# APPLE-RAISIN CRUMB PIE

1 (9-inch) pastry shell, unbaked
6 medium apples, pared and
   sliced
½ cup raisins
6 tablespoons sugar

2 tablespoons flour
1 cup sour cream
1 egg, beaten
1 teaspoon vanilla
Pinch salt

Crumb Topping:

½ cup self-rising flour
¼ cup white sugar
¼ cup brown sugar

1 teaspoon cinnamon
Sprinkle of nutmeg
⅓ cup butter

Fill unbaked pastry shell with apples and raisins mixed together. Stir sugar and flour together and fold in cream, beaten egg, vanilla and salt. You can substitute fresh cream, but sour is best. Spoon cream mixture over apples and raisins. Bake at 350 degrees for about 40 minutes, or until pie is golden brown. Combine flour, sugars, cinnamon and nutmeg. Blend in ⅓ cup butter until mixture is crumbly. Spoon crumbs over top of pie and bake 15 minutes more, or until lightly browned.

Yield: one 9-inch pie

# SOUR CREAM APPLE PIE

| | |
|---|---|
| 2 tablespoons flour | 1 cup sour cream |
| 1/8 teaspoon salt | 1 teaspoon vanilla |
| 3/4 cup sugar | 1/4 teaspoon nutmeg |
| 1 egg | 2 cups apples, diced |

Sift flour and salt. Add sugar, egg, sour cream, vanilla and nutmeg. Beat until smooth. Add apples. Pour into pastry shell. Bake at 400 degrees for 15 minutes, then at 350 degrees for 30 minutes.

**Topping:**

| | |
|---|---|
| 1/3 cup sugar | 1 teaspoon cinnamon |
| 1/3 cup flour | 1/4 cup butter |

Combine all ingredients and spread over top of pie. Return to oven and bake at 400 degrees for 10 minutes.

# SPICY APPLE PIE

| | |
|---|---|
| 3½ cups tart apples | 1/4 teaspoon nutmeg |
| 4 tablespoons all-purpose flour | 1/8 teaspoon salt |
| 1¼ cups sugar | 1 tablespoon butter |
| ½ teaspoon cinnamon | |

Make pastry for double-crust pie. Line a 9-inch pie pan or glass pie plate with pastry. Peel apples, core, cut in eights. Apples should not be sliced too thin. Combine flour, sugar, spices and salt. Spread about half of this mixture over unbaked crust bottom. Add the apples, putting the remaining dry mixture over them. Dot with butter. Cut a few slits in top crust to permit steam to escape. Fit top crust over apples removing excess pastry. Crimp edges with thumb to seal pie. Bake in preheated oven 425 degrees for 40 to 50 minutes, or until done.

Yield: one-9-inch pie

# APPLE-COCONUT PIE

**Crust:**

1 cup margarine
2 (3-ounce) packages cream
  cheese

2 cups all-purpose flour
Dash salt

Mix margarine and cream cheese; cut in flour and salt with two knives or pastry blender. Chill. Divide dough, roll half on a lightly floured board, and line a 9- or 10-inch piepan with pastry. Roll out remainder of dough for top crust and set aside. (Crust may be patted into pan rather than rolling it.)

**Filling:**

4 large, firm apples
¾ cup sugar
2 tablespoons all-purpose
  flour

½ teaspoon salt
1 (3½-ounce) can flaked coconut
1 teaspoon vanilla
2 tablespoons margarine

Peel and core apples; slice into prepared pie crust. Mix sugar, flour, and salt and sprinkle over apples. Cover with coconut, and sprinkle with vanilla. Dot with margarine. Fit top crust over pie and cut gashes in top for escape of steam. Bake at 400 degrees for 10 minutes; reduce heat to 300 degrees and cook for an additional 35 to 40 minutes.

Yield: one 9- or 10-inch pie

# DUTCH APPLE PIE

Pastry for double crust 9-inch
  pie (recipe follows)
6 cups cooking apples, peeled,
  thinly sliced
¾ cup honey
¼ cup all-purpose flour

½ teaspoon ground cinnamon
½ teaspoon ground nutmeg
Dash of salt
2 tablespoons butter or
  margarine
½ cup whipping cream

Line a 9-inch pieplate with half of pastry; set aside. Combine apples and honey, tossing gently. Combine flour, spices, and salt, stirring well; spoon over apple mixture, tossing gently. Spoon filling evenly into pastry shell, and dot with butter. Cover with top crust, and slit in several places to allow steam to escape; seal and flute edges. Cover edges of pie with aluminum foil, and bake at 425 degrees for 40 minutes. Remove the aluminum foil from edge of pie. Pour whipping cream in slits of top crust. Bake 5 additional minutes.

Yield: one 9-inch pie

**Double Crust Pastry:**

2 cups all-purpose flour
½ teaspoon salt

⅔ cup shortening
4 to 6 tablespoons cold water

Combine flour and salt; cut in shortening with pastry blender until mixture resembles coarse meal. Sprinkle cold water evenly over surface; stir with a fork until all dry ingredients are moistened. Shape dough into a ball; chill. Divide in half and roll each portion to ⅛-inch thickness on a lightly floured surface.

Yield: pastry for one double crust 9-inch pie.

# HONEY APPLE PIE

5 tart apples, peeled and sliced
½ cup sugar
3 tablespoons flour
⅓ cup whipping cream

¼ cup honey
½ teaspoon cinnamon
¼ teaspoon nutmeg
2 tablespoons butter

Line pie pan with ½ of pastry, leaving ½-inch extending over edges. Sprinkle 1 tablespoon each of sugar and flour in bottom of pastry shell. Combine remaining sugar and flour, whipping cream and honey. Pour over apples and mix lightly. Arrange apple mixture in pastry shell. Sprinkle cinnamon and nutmeg over apples; dot with butter. Cut strips ½-inch wide from remaining pastry. Make lattice top; flute edges. Bake at 400 degrees for 40 to 45 minutes.

Yield: 6 servings

# APPLE DELIGHT PIE

2 cups apples, cooked (or more
for larger pies)
Sugar, to taste
Allspice, to taste

1 cup self-rising flour (do not sift)
1 cup granulated sugar
½ cup margarine, not softened

Pour cooked apples, sweetened and spiced to taste, in pie dish. Mix together by hand the flour, sugar and margarine, leaving mixture chunky. Sprinkle over pie. Bake at 350 degrees until golden brown.

# DEEP DISH APPLE CREAM PIE

2¼ cups flour
1 teaspoon salt
⅔ cup margarine
6 or 7 tablespoons ice water
1 cup sugar

½ teaspoon ground cinnamon
⅛ teaspoon ground nutmeg
8 cups apples, sliced and peeled
1 tablespoon lemon juice
¾ cup heavy cream

Measure 2 cups flour and salt into a bowl. Cut in margarine with pastry blender or two knives until mixture resembles coarse meal. Stir in ice water; mix lightly. Form dough into a ball. Roll out ⅔ dough to fit a 10x6x1¾-inch baking dish. Transfer to baking dish. Combine sugar, remaining ¼ cup of flour, cinnamon and nutmeg. Mix with apples and lemon juice. Pile into baking dish. Roll out remaining ⅓ pastry. Cover pie; seal edges and flute. Cut several large slits in top. Bake at 425 degrees for 40 minutes. Reduce heat to 350 degrees. Remove pie from oven and pour cream through slits in top of pie. Bake 10 minutes longer.

Yield: one 10x6-inch pie.

# PASTRIES, TURNOVERS AND FRITTERS

# GOLDEN APPLE PUFFS

½ cup sugar
½ cup water
2 medium Golden Delicious
  apples
¾ cup all-purpose flour
1 teaspoon baking powder

½ teaspoon salt
¼ cup shortening
6 tablespoons milk
1 tablespoon butter
1 tablespoon sugar
¼ teaspoon cinnamon

Combine ½ cup sugar and water; bring to boil. Reduce heat and simmer 5 minutes. Peel, core and ½ apples. Place in shallow baking dish. Pour syrup over apples. Sift together flour, baking powder and salt. Cut in shortening. Add milk to make stiff dough. Top each apple half with a mound of dough, covering apple well. Make hollow in center of dough. Mix butter, sugar and cinnamon; spoon into hollows of dough. Bake at 425 degrees for 25 to 30 minutes, until apples are tender. Serve warm, with cream if desired.

Yield: 4 servings

# APPLE DELIGHT

1 cup orange juice
1 cup pineapple juice
1 (10.5-ounce) package miniature
  marshmallows

2 cups grated apples
1½ cups whipped topping
3 dozen vanilla wafers
¼ cup crushed vanilla wafers

Combine juice and marshmallows in a saucepan; cook over low heat, stirring constantly, until marshmallows melt. Chill until thick. Stir grated apples into marshmallow mixture, and fold in the whipped topping. Line a 9-inch square baking pan with whole vanilla wafers. Pour apple mixture over vanilla wafers, spreading evenly. Chill; sprinkle with crushed vanilla wafers.

Yield: 9 servings

# APPLE CRUNCH DESSERT

1 cup quick-cooking rolled oats
½ cup whole bran cereal
⅓ cup whole wheat flour
⅓ cup packed brown sugar
¼ teaspoon baking soda
½ teaspoon ground cinnamon
¼ teaspoon ground nutmeg
¼ teaspoon ground ginger

½ cup butter or margarine
1 ($3^5/8$- or 4-ounce package) regular
   butterscotch pudding mix
1½ cups milk
1 (22-ounce can) apple pie filling
1 teaspoon finely shredded lemon
   peel
2 tablespoons lemon juice

Mix oats, cereal, flour, sugar, soda and spices. Cut in butter or margarine until crumbly. Pat *half* the mixture into 8x8x2-inch baking dish. Bake in 350 degrees oven 10 minutes. Prepare pudding mix according to package directions *except* use the 1½ cups milk. Pour over crumb layer. Mix remaining ingredients; spoon over pudding. Top with remaining crumbs. Bake, uncovered, in 350 degrees oven 30 to 35 minutes. Serve warm or cool with ice cream, if desired.

Yield: 8 servings

# APPLE CRISP

8 apples, sliced
1 teaspoon cinnamon
1 teaspoon nutmeg

½ cup water
½ cup brown sugar
¾ cup flour

Arrange apples in a baking dish. Sprinkle with spices; add water. Cut butter into sugar and flour. Put mixture over apples. Bake at 350 degrees for 30 to 40 minutes.

# APPLE-DATE STRUDEL

2½ cups sifted all-purpose flour
1 teaspoon double-acting baking
  powder
½ teaspoon salt
1 egg, beaten
Butter or margarine
12 zwieback, finely rolled (about
  ¾ cup crumbs)

½ cup chopped walnuts or
  pecans
4 cups cooking aples
1 package (8-ounces) pitted dates,
  finely snipped
½ cup sugar
¼ cup lemon juice
1 teaspoon cinnamon

Sift first 3 ingredients into bowl. Add egg and ¼ cup butter, melted. Then add ½ cup ice water. Stir until blended, then knead to smooth ball on lightly floured board. Cover with towel and let rest at least ½ hour. Sauté crumbs in 2 tablespoons butter until lightly toasted, add nuts and set aside. Peel and core apples, cut in wedges, then in thin crosswise slices. Mix with next 4 ingredients. On lightly floured board, roll dough to a 24x16-inch rectangle. Brush with 2 tablespoons butter, melted. Sprinkle with crumb mixture to within 1-inch of edges. Spread evenly with apple mixture. Then roll from long side as for jelly röll and seal ends. Shape in horseshoe and put seam down, on greased baking sheet. Melt ¼ cup butter and brush some on strudel. Bake in hot oven 400 degrees, about 40 minutes. Brush occasionally with remaining butter. Serve warm in slices.

# APPLE FRITTERS

1½ cups all-purpose flour
1 tablespoon sugar
2 teaspoons baking powder
½ teaspoon salt
2 eggs, beaten
⅔ cup milk

1 tablespoon salad oil
3 cups apples, peeled and
  finely chopped
Hot salad oil
Powdered sugar

Combine dry ingredients in a bowl; add eggs, milk, salad oil and apples. Stir just until moistened. Drop batter by spoonfuls into ½-inch hot oil. Cook until golden brown (about 3 to 4 minutes on each side); drain. Roll fritters in powdered sugar.

Yield: about 3 dozen

# APPLE PUFFS

6 large apples
Orange marmalade
¼ cup butter or margarine
½ cup brown sugar

3 teaspoons cinnamon
1 teaspoon allspice
1 teaspoon nutmeg
Pie dough pastry

Pare and core apples. Fill centers with orange marmalade. Make a paste by combining the butter or margarine, brown sugar and spices. Cover apples completely with the paste. Prepare pie dough pastry from a favorite recipe and wrap each apple in pastry. Place apples on cookie sheet or casserole and bake in a 325 degrees oven for about 1 hour. Serve hot with rum sauce.

Rum Sauce:

2 tablespoons butter
¼ cup powdered sugar
½ teaspoon grated orange peel
½ cup whipping cream (or
   whipped topping)

2 tablespoons rum (or 1
   teaspoon rum flavoring)

Cream together the butter, powdered sugar and orange peel. Beat whipping cream until stiff. Fold into creamed mixture. Add rum last.

Yield: 6 servings

*Mrs. R.L. Maples*
*Gatlinburg, Tennessee*

# APPLE DUMPLINGS

2 cups all-purpose flour
2 teaspoons baking powder
1 teaspoon salt
1 tablespoon butter or margarine,
   softened
1 tablespoon shortening
1 cup milk

½ cup butter or margarine,
   melted
1 teaspoon ground cinnamon
4 tablespoons brown sugar
6 tart apples, peeled, cored
   and chopped
Apple Dumpling Sauce

Combine flour, baking powder and salt in a large mixing bowl. Cut in butter and shortening until mixture resembles coarse meal. Gradually add milk to make a soft dough. Roll dough into a ¼-inch thick rectangle on a lightly floured surface. Brush with melted butter; sprinkle with cinnamon and brown sugar. Spread apples over pastry. Roll up jellyroll fashion; cut into 10 slices. Place flat in a greased 13x9x2-inch baking pan; bake at 350 degrees for 20 minutes. Pour Apple Dumpling Sauce over top, and continue baking 20 minutes.

Yield: 10 servings

**Apple Dumpling Sauce:**

1 cup sugar
1 tablespoon all-purpose flour
Dash of salt

1 tablespoon butter or margarine
½ teaspoon lemon juice
1 cup hot water

Combine all ingredients in a saucepan over medium heat. Bring to a boil; cook 2 minutes, stirring constantly.

Yield: 1½ cups

# APPLE-NUT CRUNCH

½ cup all-purpose flour
2 teaspoons baking powder
½ teaspoon salt
2 eggs
1 cup light brown sugar, packed

1 teaspoon vanilla extract
1 cup pecans, chopped
1 cup tart apples, peeled and
 cubed
Sweetened whipped cream

Combine flour, baking powder and salt; set aside. Beat eggs and sugar until light and fluffy. Add flour mixture to egg mixture; blending well. Stir in vanilla, pecans and apples. Spread mixture in a greased 10-inch pieplate. Bake at 350 degrees for 30 minutes. Cool; cut into wedges, and serve with sweetened whipped cream.

Yield: 8 servings


# APPLE-CINNAMON PUFFS

1 cup sugar
1 cup water
½ teaspoon red food coloring
 (optional)
4 to 5 tart apples, peeled and
 thinly sliced
1½ cups all-purpose flour
2 teaspoons baking powder

½ teaspoon salt
¼ cup shortening
¾ cup milk
2 tablespoons melted margarine
2 tablespoons sugar
½ teaspoon ground cinnamon
Cream or half-and-half (optional)

Combine sugar and water in a saucepan; add coloring, if desired. Bring to a boil over medium heat. Boil about 5 minutes, stirring constantly. Set aside. Place apples in a greased 12x8x2-inch baking dish. Pour sugar syrup over apples. Combine flour, baking powder and salt; cut in shortening with a pastry blender until mixture resembles small peas. Gradually add milk, stirring with a fork until well moistened. Drop dough by heaping tablespoonfuls on top of apples. With a moistened fingertip, make a small indention on top of each spoonful. Melt margarine in a saucepan; add sugar and cinnamon, stirring until sugar is dissolved. Spoon mixture evenly into the indentions. Bake at 425 degrees for 30 minutes. Serve warm with cream, if desired.

Yield: 8 to 10 servings

# LAZY APPLE STRUDEL

¾ cup butter or margarine,
   melted
1 cup milk
2 egg yolks
3½ cups all-purpose flour
Melted butter or margarine
5 to 6 large cooking apples,
   peeled and sliced

½ cup raisins, divided
½ cup chopped pecans, divided
½ cup flaked coconut, divided
1 cup sugar, divided
Ground cinnamon

Combine ¾ cup butter, milk, egg yolks and flour; blend well. Chill dough at least 2 hours. Divide dough into 2 parts; roll each part out on a floured surface to a 12x18-inch rectangle. Brush surface with melted butter. Arrange ½ the apple slices in center of each rectangle in a single layer, leaving a 2-inch border without apples. Sprinkle ½ the raisins, pecans, coconut and sugar over apples on each rectangle. Sprinkle cinnamon over all. Starting with long edge, roll up jellyroll fashion, turning in ends as you roll. Place strudels on a greased jellyroll pan, seam-side down. Bake at 350 degrees for 1 hour.

Yield: two 14-inch strudels

# APPLE CRUNCH

¾ cup sifted flour
¾ teaspoon salt
1 teaspoon cinnamon
1 cup sugar

½ cup butter
6 medium cooking apples, 6 cups
½ cup coarsely chopped walnuts

Into a medium mixing bowl, sift together flour, salt, cinnamon and sugar. With a pastry blender thoroughly cut in butter until mixture looks like crumbs. Peel, core and cut apples into eighths; slice crosswise thinly. Turn apples into a rectangular 11x7x1½-inch baking pan, sprinkle with walnuts; put flour mixture on top. (Pan will be very full, but apples will sink during baking.) Bake in preheated 350 degrees oven until apples are tender, about 55 minutes. Test apples by piercing with a fork. Remove from oven; place under broiler to brown top lightly. Serve warm with whipped topping or ice cream.

Yield: 8 servings.

# APPLE SWIRL

½ cup butter or margarine
2 cups sugar
2 cups water
1½ cups sifted self-rising flour

½ cup shortening
⅓ cup milk
2 cups apples, finely chopped
1 teaspoon cinnamon

Melt butter in a 13x9x2-inch baking dish or sheet cake pan. In a saucepan, heat sugar and water until sugar melts. Cut shortening into flour until particles are like fine crumbs. Add milk and stir with a fork only until dough leaves the side of the bowl. Turn out onto lightly floured board or pastry cloth, knead just until smooth. Roll dough out into a large rectangle about ¼-inch thick. Sprinkle cinnamon over apples; then sprinkle apples evenly over the dough. Roll up dough like a jellyroll. Dampen the edge of dough with a little water and seal. Slice dough into about 16 slices, ½-inch thick. Place in a pan with melted butter. Pour sugar syrup carefully around rolls. (This looks like too much liquid, but the crust will absorb it.) Bake at 350 degrees for 1 hour.

Yield: 8 servings.

# APPLE MERINGUE

4 to 6 medium tart apples, peeled
  and cored
¼ cup butter, melted
⅓ cup white seedless raisins,
  plumped

⅔ cup sugar
2 tablespoons fresh lemon juice
3 egg whites
½ teaspoon salt

Slice apples about ¼-inch thick. Place in a well buttered baking dish. Pour melted butter over apples. Sprinkle with raisins, lemon juice and ½ of the sugar. Cover with aluminum foil and bake at 350 degrees for about 20 minutes, or until apples are tender. Beat egg whites with salt until stiff. Gradually add the remaining sugar to make a stiff meringue. Spread meringue over apples to the edge of dish. Bake an additional 10 minutes, or until meringue is brown. Serve warm. Cream may be added if desired.

Yield: 4 to 6 servings

# APPLE TURNOVERS

1 cup unsifted flour
½ teaspoon salt
⅓ cup margarine
1 package (3-ounces) cream cheese
1½ cups apples, peeled
   and chopped

¼ cup sugar
¼ teaspoon ground cinnamon
Dash nutmeg
Powdered sugar

Measure flour and salt into a bowl. Cut in margarine and cream cheese with pastry blender or two knives until mixture resembles coarse meal. Mix with hands until dough forms a ball. Chill 1 hour. On lightly floured board roll chilled dough to 12x16-inch rectangle. Cut into twelve 4-inch squares. Combine apples, sugar, cinnamon and nutmeg; mix well. Place 1 rounded teaspoonful of apple mixture in center of each square. Moisten 2 adjacent sides of each square and fold to form triangles; seal edges with tines of fork. Cut 2 small slits in top of each turnover. Place on ungreased baking sheets. Bake at 400 degrees about 15 minutes, or until lightly browned. Remove from baking sheets and cool on wire racks. Sprinkle with powdered sugar.

Yield: 12 servings

# APPLE RINGS

½ cup white sugar
1 cup brown sugar

½ cup butter
1½ cups water

Mix sugar, butter and water; pour in baking dish. Place in oven and bring to boil.

1½ cups flour
½ cup shortening
3 teaspoons water, or less

4 cups apples, grated
Cinnamon

Mix dough and roll thin. Spread with 4 cups grated apples; sprinkle with cinnamon. Roll up and cut in 1-inch rolls. Put in baking dish and bake at 400 degrees for 30 to 35 minutes.

*Loretta Kilpatrick*
*Greenback, Tennessee*

# PUDDINGS

# BAKED APPLE RICE PUDDING

2 slightly beaten egg yolks
2 medium apples, peeled, cored, and finely chopped (2 cups)
1½ cups cooked rice
½ cup milk
½ cup pitted whole dates, chopped

¼ cup sugar
2 tablespoons butter or margarine, melted
1 teaspoon vanilla
2 egg whites

In bowl stir together egg yolks, apples, cooked rice, milk, dates, sugar, butter or margarine, and vanilla. Beat egg whites to stiff peaks (tips stand up). Fold egg whites into apple mixture. Turn into a 1½-quart soufflé dish. Place in a larger baking pan. Set on oven rack. Pour boiling water into larger pan to a depth of 1 inch. Bake in 325 degrees oven for 70 to 75 minutes. Serve warm or chilled. Garnish with fresh apple slices dipped in lemon juice, if desired.

Yield: 6 servings

# SMOKY MOUNTAIN APPLE PUDDING

3½ tablespoons all-purpose flour
½ cup sugar
4 teaspoons baking powder
⅛ teaspoon salt
1 egg, separated

1 tablespoon vanilla
½ cup pecans, chopped
½ cup apples, peeled and
   chopped

Sift together flour, sugar, baking powder and salt; set aside. In another bowl, beat egg white until stiff. Fold in egg yolk and vanilla, then flour mixture, until well combined. Stir in chopped pecans and apples. Pour batter into 4 greased and floured custard cups. Bake in a preheated 350 degrees oven for 15 to 20 minutes, or until evenly and lightly browned on top. Remove to a cooling rack.

Yield: 4 individual servings

# BAKED APPLE PUDDING

⅓ cup margarine, softened
1 cup sugar
1 egg
1 cup unsifted all-purpose flour
1 teaspoon baking soda
¼ teaspoon salt

¼ teaspoon ground nutmeg
¼ teaspoon ground cinnamon
1 teaspoon vanilla extract
2 cups apples, grated and
   unpared
½ cup walnuts, chopped

Combine margarine, sugar and egg in mixer bowl; beat until light. Gradually blend in combined flour, baking soda, salt, nutmeg and cinnamon. Stir in vanilla, apples and walnuts. Turn mixture into an ungreased 8-inch square baking pan. Bake at 350 degrees, or until done. Serve warm or cold topped with whipped cream or ice cream.

Yield: 8 to 10 servings

# CARAMEL APPLE BREAD PUDDING

28 Caramels
¼ cup water
4 cups bread cubes
4 cups apples, peeled and sliced
5 eggs, slightly beaten

2 cups milk
¼ cup sugar
1 teaspoon vanilla
¼ teaspoon salt
¼ teaspoon cinnamon

Melt caramels with water in a covered double boiler or in a saucepan over low heat. Stir occasionally until sauce is smooth. Place bread cubes in greased 11¾x7½-inch baking dish. Top with apple slices. Combine eggs, milk, sugar, vanilla, salt and cinnamon; pour over apples. Cover with caramel sauce. Set dish in large pan on oven rack; pour in boiling water to ½-inch depth. Bake at 325 degrees for 1 hour and 20 minutes or until knife inserted halfway between center and outside edge comes out clean. Serve hot or cold.

Yield: 8 to 10 servings

# SALADS

# APPLE CIDER MOLD

3 cups apple cider
2 envelopes unflavored gelatin
¼ cup sugar
1 can (6-ounces) frozen lemonade
    concentrate

2 large red apples, skinned
    and diced
¼ cup chopped celery
¼ cup slivered almonds
Whipped cream for topping

Mix 1 cup cider with gelatin in small pan. Let stand for few minutes.
Add sugar and cook; stir until dissolved, remove from heat. Core and
dice apples and mix with thawed lemonade concentrate to prevent any
darkening. Lift out apples with slotted spoon and reserve. Stir lemonade
and remaining cider into gelatin mixture. Refrigerate until thick and
syrupy, then add apples and celery. Place almonds or other chopped nuts
in bottom of 6-cup mold. Spoon gelatin over nuts, cover and chill firm.
Dip mold to the rim in hot water for 5 seconds to invert onto serving
plate. Surround with lettuce leaves and serve with whipped cream. Sour
cream goes good with this, too.

# WALDORF SALAD

3 large Winesap apples
1 tablespoon lemon juice
1 cup chopped celery
½ cup coarsely chopped walnuts
    or pecans

½ cup raisins
½ cup salad dressing

Peel and dice apples. Sprinkle with lemon juice; add celery and raisins
and toss together. Cover and chill. Just before serving, add nuts and
salad dressing. Toss lightly to distribute dressing. Serve on crisp lettuce
cups or from salad bowl.

# APPLE CIDER SALAD

1 (6-ounce) package orange-
   flavored gelatin
4 cups apple cider
1 cup raisins
1 cup apples, coarsely chopped

1 cup celery, chopped
Juice and grated rind of 1 lemon
Lettuce
1 apple, unpeeled and sliced

Dissolve gelatin in 2 cups hot cider; stir in raisins. Let cool. Add remaining 2 cups cider; chill until consistency of unbeaten egg whites. Stir in chopped apples, celery, lemon juice and rind. Pour into a lightly oiled 6 cup mold. Chill until set. Unmold onto lettuce leaves and garnish with apple slices, if desired.

Yield: 8 to 10 servings

*Georgia Kilpatrick*
*Sevierville, Tennessee*

# KRAUT AND APPLE SALAD

1 quart chopped kraut, drained
1 large apple, chopped
1 cup celery, chopped
1 cup onion, chopped

1 cup sweet pepper, chopped
   (1 green and 1 red)
1 cup sugar
½ cup vinegar

Combine all ingredients and mix well. Let set at least 4 hours. Keeps well.

# SUNSHINE APPLE ASPIC

3 envelopes unflavored gelatin
1 cup cold water
3 cups boiling water
¾ cup sugar
1½ teaspoons salt
⅓ cup cider vinegar
½ cup lime juice

2 large sweet apples, unpeeled
  and chopped
1 large green pepper, chopped
½ cup green onion, chopped
Lettuce
Apple slices

Soften gelatin in cold water. Add boiling water, sugar and salt; stir until gelatin is dissolved. Stir in vinegar and lime juice; chill until consistency of unbeaten egg white. Fold in apples, green pepper and onion. Spoon into a lightly oiled 9x5x3-inch loaf pan; chill until firm. Unmold on lettuce, and garnish with apple slices.

Yield: 8 to 10 servings

# FRESH APPLE SALAD

1½ cups apples, chopped
1 cup celery, coarsely chopped
½ cup raisins
2 tablespoons mayonnaise

1 tablespoon sugar
⅛ teaspoon salt
Dash of pepper

Combine apples, celery and raisins. Combine mayonnaise, sugar, salt and pepper; stir well. Pour over apple mixture; toss gently.

Yield: 4 to 6 servings

# WALNUT APPLE SALAD

¼ cup olive or vegetable oil
2 tablespoons cider vinegar
2 tablespoons lemon juice
½ teaspoon sugar
¼ teaspoon salt
½ teaspoon Worcestershire sauce

¼ cup crumbled bleu cheese
2 cups broken lettuce
1 cup celery, sliced
½ cup walnuts, broken
¼ cup raisins
3 cups eating apples

Combine oil, vinegar, lemon juice, sugar, salt, Worcestershire sauce and bleu cheese in jar with tight-fitting cover. Shake well to blend; chill. Place lettuce in large bowl with celery, walnuts and raisins; cover and place in refrigerator to keep chilled until serving time. Wash, quarter and core apples; cut into bite-size chunks; add to salad bowl. Pour bleu cheese dressing over salad; toss lightly to mix.

Yield: 6 servings

# CHICKEN-APPLE SALAD

2 cups chicken, cooked and diced
2 cups apples, unpared and diced
½ cup celery, chopped
¼ cup raisins

1 tablespoon lemon juice
½ cup salad dressing or
  mayonnaise
6 lettuce cups

Mix all ingredients except lettuce. Chill thoroughly. Serve in lettuce cups.

Yield: 6 servings, ⅔ cup each

# FRUIT COMPOTE

1 can (15¼-ounce) Pineapple
   Chunks in its own juice, chilled
2 oranges
2 apples

2 bananas
½ cup mayonnaise
½ cup dairy sour cream
2 tablespoons honey

Drain pineapple, reserving juice. Pare oranges and slice thinly. Slice apples into thin wedges. Slice bananas. Dip apples and bananas in reserved juice to prevent browning. Arrange fruits in compote. Combine 2 tablespoons reserved pineapple juice, mayonnaise, sour cream and honey. Mix well. Serve over fruit.

Yield: 6 to 8 servings

# WALDORF SALAD MOLD

1 package (3-ounce) lemon gelatin
½ teaspoon salt
1 cup boiling water
¾ cup cold water
2 teaspoons vinegar

¾ cup finely diced celery
1 cup diced red apples
¼ cup chopped walnuts
¼ cup mayonnaise (optional)

Dissolve gelatin and salt in boiling water. Add cold water and vinegar. Chill until very thick. Fold in celery, apples, walnuts and mayonnaise. Spoon into individual molds or a 1-quart mold. Chill until firm. Unmold and serve with cream cheese or whipped topping.

# SWEET BREADS AND MUFFINS

# APPLE-NUT BREAD

2 cups sugar
4 eggs, beaten
4 cups all-purpose flour
2 teaspoons soda
1 teaspoon salt
1 cup salad oil

¼ cup commercial sour cream
2 cups apples, peeled and
  chopped
1 cup pecans, chopped
1 teaspoon vanilla extract

Gradually add sugar to eggs; beat until light and fluffy. Combine dry ingredients; add to sugar mixture alternately with oil and sour cream, beating well after each addition. Stir in apples, pecans and vanilla. Spoon batter into 2 greased and floured 9¼x5¼x2¾-inch loaf pans. Bake at 350 degrees for 1 hour or until toothpick inserted in center comes out clean. Let cool in pans 5 minutes; turn out on wire racks to finish cooling.

Yield: 2 loaves

# FRESH APPLE BREAD

1 cup sugar
½ cup shortening
2 eggs, beaten
1 cup tart apples, ground or
  grated
2 cups sifted all-purpose flour
½ teaspoon salt

1 teaspoon soda
1 cup broken pecan pieces
1½ tablespoons buttermilk
½ teaspoon vanilla
3 tablespoons sugar
1 teaspoon cinnamon

Cream sugar and shortening; add eggs and apples. Sift dry ingredients together. Mix with sugar mixture; add pecans. Stir in buttermilk and vanilla. Pour into greased 10x6x3-inch loaf pan. Mix sugar and cinnamon; sprinkle over top. Bake for 1 hour at 350 degrees.

Yield: 1 loaf

# APPLE-DAPPLE LOAF

¼ cup shortening
⅔ cup sugar
2 eggs
2 cups all-purpose flour
1 teaspoon baking powder

1 teaspoon soda
1 teaspoon salt
2 cups raw apples, grated
½ cup nuts, chopped

Beat shortening, sugar and eggs together until light and fluffy. Sift dry ingredients together; add alternately with grated apples. Add nuts. The batter will be stiff. Turn into greased and floured loaf pan. Bake at 350 degrees for about 1 hour.

# APPLE BUTTERSCOTCH MUFFINS

3 cups self-rising flour
¼ cup sugar
2 eggs, beaten
1½ cups milk

⅓ cup salad oil
1 (6-ounce) package butterscotch
 chips
1 cup apples, peeled and diced

Combine flour and sugar. Combine remaining ingredients; add all at once to flour mixture, stirring only until flour is moistened. Fill greased muffin cups ⅔ full. Bake at 425 degrees for 20 to 25 minutes, or until golden brown.

Yield: 18 muffins

# APPLE WHOLE WHEAT WAFFLES

2 cups whole wheat flour
½ teaspoon salt
1 tablespoon sugar
1 tablespoon baking powder
½ teaspoon ground cinnamon
½ teaspoon ground nutmeg
¼ teaspoon cloves

⅔ cup dry milk solids
2 eggs
⅓ cup salad oil
1 teaspoon vanilla extract
1 medium apple, cored, peeled
 and chopped
1¾ cups apple juice

Combine first 7 ingredients. Place remaining ingredients in container of electric blender; blend until apple is pureed. Combine liquid ingredients and dry ingredients, mixing well. Bake in a preheated waffle iron.

Yield: 8 waffles

# APPLE-CORNMEAL MUFFINS

1½ cups sifted all-purpose flour
⅓ cup sugar
3 teaspoons baking powder
½ teaspoon salt
1 cup yellow cornmeal

1 cup milk
1 egg, beaten
1 cup tart green summer apples,
   cored, pared, and finely
   chopped

Sift together flour, sugar, baking powder, and salt; stir in cornmeal. Combine milk and egg. Add to flour mixture along with the chopped apples. Stir quickly just until dry ingredients are moistened. Fill greased 2½-inch muffin pans ⅔ full. Bake in 400 degrees oven for 20 to 25 minutes.

Yield: 12 to 15 muffins

# AUTUMN APPLE BREAD

¼ cup shortening
⅔ cup sugar
2 eggs, beaten
2 cups sifted all-purpose flour
1 teaspoon baking powder

1 teaspoon salt
2 cups apples, coarsely grated,
   peeled raw
1 tablespoon grated lemon peel
⅔ cup nuts, chopped

Cream shortening and sugar until light and fluffy; beat in eggs. Sift next 4 ingredients. Add alternately with apples to egg mixture. Stir in lemon rind and nuts. Bake in floured, greased 9x5x3-inch loaf pan in preheated 350 degrees oven for approximately 40 to 50 minutes. Cool before slicing.

Yield: 1 loaf

# APPLE PAN BREAD

1 cup sifted all-purpose flour
2½ teaspoons baking powder
½ teaspoon salt
¼ cup sugar
2 cups raisin bran flakes
⅔ cup milk

1 egg
¼ cup soft vegetable shortening
½ cup sugar
½ teaspoon ground cinnamon
2 cups thinly sliced, pared,
  cooking apples

Sift together flour, baking powder, salt and ¼ cup sugar. Set aside. Combine bran flakes and milk, add egg and shortening; beat well. Add sifted dry ingredients; stir only until blended, but do not beat. Spread in a greased 8x8x2-inch pan. Mix together ½ cup sugar and ½ teaspoon cinnamon. Dip apple slices in mixture; arrange on top of batter. Sprinkle any remaining sugar mixture over apple slices. Bake at 400 degrees about 30 minutes. Cut in squares and serve warm.

Yield: nine 2½-inch squares

# APPLE-CHEESE BREAD

½ cup soft shortening
½ cup sugar
2 eggs
1½ cups sifted all-purpose flour
1 teaspoon baking powder
1 teaspoon soda

½ teaspoon salt
2 tablespoons milk
¾ cup rolled oats, uncooked
1 cup raw apples, finely chopped
⅔ cup cheese, coarsely grated
½ cup nut meats, chopped

Beat shortening until creamy; gradually add sugar. Add eggs; beat well. Sift together flour, baking powder, soda and salt. Add to egg mixture with milk and stir only until blended. Add oats, apples, cheese and nut meats, all at once. Stir lightly. Batter will be very stiff. Place in greased pound loaf pan. Bake at 350 degrees about 50 minutes.

# APPLE PECAN MUFFINS

1 cup rolled oats
1 cup buttermilk
1 cup apples, grated
½ cup pecans, chopped
3 tablespoons butter or
  margarine

3 tablespoons shortening
½ cup brown sugar
1 egg
1 cup all-purpose flour
½ teaspoon baking powder
½ teaspoon salt

In a large bowl, stir oats into buttermilk; let soak 10 minutes. Add grated apples and pecans; set aside. In another bowl, cream butter, shortening and brown sugar; beat in egg. Combine with oat mixture. Sift together flour, baking powder, salt, and add oat mixture, stirring just until all ingredients are combined. The batter should be very lumpy. Divide batter between 12 well greased muffin tins and bake in a pre-heated 400 degrees oven for 25 to 30 minutes, or until evenly browned. Remove from tins and serve.

Yield: 12 muffins

# MARVELOUS APPLE MUFFINS

2 cups sifted all-purpose flour
2 tablespoons sugar
1 tablespoon baking powder
½ teaspoon salt
1 cup milk
1 egg, beaten

¼ cup butter or margarine
½ cup apples, peeled and
  chopped
¼ cup sugar
½ teaspoon ground cinnamon

Combine first 4 ingredients in a small mixing bowl; make a well in center of mixture. Combine milk, egg and butter; add to flour mixture stirring, just until moistened. Fill greased muffin tins ⅔ full; top with chopped apples. Combine ¼ cup sugar and cinnamon; sprinkle 1 teaspoon sugar mixture over each muffin. Bake at 425 degrees for 25 minutes, or until lightly browned.

Yield: 12 muffins

# CHEESY APPLE SALAD

3 medium apples, unpeeled and
  cut into thin wedges
2 cups sliced celery
1 (20-ounce) can pineapple
  chunks, drained
1 (8-ounce) package sharp
  Cheddar cheese, cubed

¾ cup slivered almonds,
  toasted
¼ cup commercial sour cream
½ cup mayonnaise
Leaf lettuce (optional)

Combine first 5 ingredients in a mixing bowl; set aside.

Combine sour cream and mayonnaise; mix well. Pour over apple mixture; toss gently to mix. Chill 1 to 2 hours; serve on lettuce-lined plates, if desired.

Yield: 10 servings

# CANDIED YAM WITH CIDER

3 large yams
¾ cup unpasteurized cider

⅓ cup brown sugar
2 tablespoons butter

Topping:

2 tablespoons brown sugar
2 tablespoons flour

1 tablespoon butter

Cook yams in boiling water about 20 minutes, until barely tender. Peel and cut in half lengthwise. Arrange in buttered baking dish. In saucepan combine cider, brown sugar and butter, bring to boil and simmer for 10 minutes. Pour over yams in baking dish and bake at 375 degrees for 45 minutes. Baste yams several times during the baking with the syrup. Mix topping ingredients, sprinkle over yams, turn oven up to 400 degrees and bake 15 minutes.

# CELERY SEED DRESSING
*For Fruit Plate and House Dressing*

Add to fruit plate just before serving. This dressing may be made with an electric blender or mixer. Constant beating, in any case, is a prerequisite.

Combine:

½ cup sugar                          1 teaspoon salt
1 teaspoon dry mustard               1 or 2 teaspoons celery seed

Add:

1 tablespoon grated onion


Gradually add, beating constantly:

1 cup vegetable oil                  ⅓ cup vinegar

Garnish with:

(A few finely cut sprigs of lemon thyme)

Yield: 2 cups


# APPLEWOOD FRESH FRUIT SALAD

1 fresh pineapple, peeled, cored,      4 oranges peeled and
   and cubed                              sectioned
1 quart fresh strawberries           2 bananas sliced
½ cup fresh blueberries (may use     1 cup sugar
   frozen, thawed)                   1 teaspoon almond extract
½ cup fresh raspberries              1 teaspoon vanilla extract
2 cups Red delicious apples          2 cups orange juice
   chopped unpeeled

Combine fruit in a large bowl. Combine remaining ingredients, stirring until sugar dissolves. Pour over fruit mixture, tossing lightly. Chill 2 to 3 hours.

Yields 14 to 16 servings.

# APPLESAUCE MUFFINS

1 cup butter
2 cups sugar
2 eggs, beaten
2 cups applesauce
2 teaspoons soda

4 cups plain flour
1 tablespoon cinnamon
1 tablespoon allspice
2 tablespoons vanilla extract

Preheat oven to 350 degrees. Cream butter and sugar; add beaten eggs. Heat applesauce; stir in soda. Add alternately with sifted flour, spices and vanilla to creamed mixture. Bake in greased muffin tins until light brown, approximately 15 to 20 minutes. Batter will keep, covered, in refrigerator for several days.

# APPLE CRANBERRY CRISP
*Good enough for company*

4 medium sized cooking apples
   (about 1⅓ pounds)
1 (1-pound) can whole cranberry
   sauce
1 teaspoon cinnamon

1 cup uncooked quick rolled oats
1 cup flour
1 cup dark brown sugar
   (firmly packed)
½ cup butter

Peel apples and slice thin. Arrange in square baking dish about 10x6-inch. Sprinkle with cinnamon. Spoon cranberry sauce over this. Stir rolled oats, flour and brown sugar together. Cut in butter until evenly mixed and crumbly. Sprinkle over cranberry layer. Bake in moderate oven—350 degrees—until apples are cooked through and top is lightly browned. About 40 minutes. Serve hot with whipped cream, or vanilla ice cream.

Yield: 8 servings

# HORSERADISH SAUCE

½ cup whipping cream
¼ cup mayonnaise
2 tablespoons salad mustard
1 heaping tablespoon horseradish

½ teaspoon lemon juice
½ teaspoon Worcestershire sauce
¼ teaspoon seasoned salt
⅛ teaspoon each salt, pepper

Beat cream until stiff. Fold in rest of ingredients. Chill. Serve with brisket and sausages.

Yield: 1 cup

# CHICKEN ALA ORCHARD

3 boneless chicken breast (or 12
   Chicken Tenders)
16 chunks pineapple

1 apple in chunks
2 peaches in slices
2 apricots in slices

Sauté chicken in a skillet with butter after cutting into bite size portions. Sauté 2 slices of onion for five minutes, remove onions and sauté fruit. Combine chicken with fruit and cover with 2 ounces of sauce.

Sauce:

Combine 1 cup orange juice
¼ cup honey
2 tablespoons lemon juice

½ teaspoon ground curry powder
1 teaspoon salt

Warm sauce

Yield: 4 servings

# SALMONBURGERS

Sauce:

⅓ cup mayonnaise or dairy
   sour cream

¼ teaspoon grated lemon peel
⅛ teaspoon dried dill weed

Patties:
1 can (16 ounces) Salmon,
   drained, cleaned and
   flaked
½ cup finely shredded
   Cheddar cheese
⅓ cup fine dry bread crumbs
   (unseasoned)
¼ cup chopped celery

¼ cup mayonnaise or dairy
   sour cream
1 egg
2 tablespoons chopped green
   onion
½ teaspoon prepared mustard
⅛ teaspoon garlic powder
⅛ teaspoon pepper

For sauce: in small bowl combine all ingredients. Set aside.

For patties: In medium mixing bowl combine all ingredients. Sauté 8 to 10 minutes on each side.

# APPLEWOOD'S SPECIAL PIE CAKE

¼ cup butter or margarine,
   softened
1 cup sugar
1 egg
1 cup all-purpose flour
1 teaspoon salt
1 teaspoon ground cinnamon

2 tablespoons hot water
1 teaspoon vanilla extract
3 cups peeled, diced cooking
   apples
½ cup chopped pecans
Rum Butter Sauce
Whipped cream (optional)

Cream butter; gradually add sugar, beating well at medium speed of an electric mixer. Add egg; beat until blended. Combine flour, salt, and cinnamon; mix well. Add to creamed mixture; beat on low speed of an electric mixer; beat on low speed of an electric mixer until smooth. Stir in water and vanilla. Fold in apples and pecans; spoon into a greased and floured 9-inch pieplate. Bake at 350 degrees for 45 minutes or until a wooden pick inserted in center comes out clean. Serve warm or cold with Rum-Butter Sauce and whipped cream if desired.

**Rum-Butter Sauce:**

½ cup firmly packed brown sugar
½ cup sugar
¼ cup butter or margarine,
   softened

½ cup whipping cream
2 tablespoons rum

Combine first 4 ingredients in a small saucepan; mix well. Bring to a boil, and cook 1 minute. Stir in rum.

Serve with a dollop of whipped cream made of:

1 pint whipping cream
⅓ cup brown sugar

1 teaspoon vanilla

# APPLEWOOD FRIED BISCUITS

1 quart milk
¼ cup of sugar
2⅔ packages dry yeast

½ cup shortening
3 teaspoons of salt
7 to 9 cups of flour

Add yeast to warm water. Add other ingredients and let dough rise. Work into biscuits and let drop into hot fat.

This recipe will make about seven dozen biscuits. They can be frozen individually and stored in plastic bags. When you work them up, don't let the biscuits rise too high. The fat should be slightly hotter than 350 degrees F. If the fat should be too hot, the biscuits will sag in the center.

# APPLE CIDER PIE

2 cups apple cider
6 (2 to 3 inch) cinnamon sticks
8 cups sliced, peeled cooking
  apples
1 tablespoon lemon juice
1 cup dried mixed fruit bits

⅔ cup sugar
2 tablespoons all-purpose flour
3 tablespoons butter or
  margarine
2 tablespoons honey
1 tablespoon cornstarch

Prepare pastry. Bring cider and cinnamon to boiling. Boil gently uncovered 20 minutes or till reduced to one cup. Strain through cheesecloth-lined sieve. Discard cinnamon. Set aside.

For filling if apples lack tartness sprinkle with lemon juice. In saucepan combine 2 tablespoons cider mixture and apples. Cook covered 4 to 5 minutes or till tender but not soft. Remove from heat. Add fruit bits, toss. Combine sugar and flour, stir into apples. Divide pastry in half, for bottom crust on lightly floured surface, roll half of the dough into a 12 inch circle, fit into a 9 inch pie plate. Trim pastry even with rim. Turn filling into pastry, dot with 1 tablespoon butter. For top crust, roll remaining dough on flour surface into 12 inch circle, make cutouts, trim to ½ inch beyond edge. Seal and flute edge high. Brush with milk, sprinkle with sugar. Cover edge of pie with foil. Bake in a 375 degree oven for 25 minutes. Remove foil, bake about 20 minutes or more or till crust is golden, cool.

To serve, prepare sauce in a saucepan. Combine remaining cider mixture, 2 tablespoons butter, honey and cornstarch, cook and stir till bubbly, cook and stir 2 minutes more. Serve pie with ice cream and warm sauce.

# APPLE FRITTERS

1 cup milk
1 egg (beaten)
4 tablespoons margarine
¼ cup sugar
½ teaspoon salt
1 orange, rind and juice

1 cup apples (chopped but not
  *too* fine)
3 cups cake flour
2 teaspoons baking powder
1 teaspoon vanilla

Beat egg. In a mixing bowl, combine the milk, egg and melted margarine. Add the orange juice, rind, chopped apples (skins can be left on) and vanilla. Sift together the flour, salt, baking powder. Stir into milk mixture with a spoon until blended. *Do not overmix.* Preheat oil in a skillet to 350 degrees. Drop off end of tablespoon into hot oil. Fry to a golden brown. Turn so they brown evenly. Allow to cool.

# APPLEWOOD JULEP

1 quart unsweetened apple juice,
  chilled
1 cup unsweetened pineapple
  juice, chilled

1 cup orange juice, chilled
¼ cup lemon juice, chilled
Fresh mint sprigs

Combine first 4 ingredients with ice cubes; mix well. Garnish servings
with mint.

Yield: 6¼ cups


# APPLE CHEESE PIE

2 eggs
1 cup cottage cheese
1 cup sugar
⅛ teaspoon salt
1 cup cream
1 teaspoon vanilla

1½ cups tart apples, thinly sliced
⅛ teaspoon nutmeg and
  cinnamon
Mild yellow cheese, shredded
  or grated
½ cup whipped cream

Beat eggs. Add cottage cheese, ½ cup sugar, salt, cream, and vanilla.
Line an 8-inch pie plate with pastry. Combine apples with ½ cup sugar
and spices. (The amount of sugar may vary depending on the tartness
of apples.) Turn apples into pastry. Cover with cottage cheese mixture.
Bake for 35 minutes (400 degrees for 10 minutes and 350 degrees for 25
minutes) until cottage cheese mixture is set. Remove from oven and let
cool. Top with whipped cream or ice cream.

**Cream Cheese Pastry:**

½ cup butter
1 (3-ounce) package cream
  cheese

1¼ cups flour, sifted
⅛ teaspoon salt

Cream butter and cream cheese together. Sift flour once, measure, add
salt and cut into cheese mixture until it resembles a fine meal. Wrap in
waxed paper, press firmly together; chill. When mixture is chilled, roll
⅛ inch thick on a lightly floured pastry canvas. Fit into pie pan or plate.
Bake in a 400 degree oven for 12 to 15 minutes.

Yield: 8 servings

# MARGARET'S CARAMEL PIE

1 pie crust–cooked

Mix and cook in double boiler until thick the following:

1 cup brown sugar
½ cup flour

2 cups milk
3 egg yolks

Add:

⅓ cup butter

1 teaspoon vanilla

Top with meringue made of:

3 egg whites
1 tablespoon cornstarch

3 tablespoons sugar
1 teaspoon vanilla

Put in oven at 350 degrees. Brown until golden.

Yield: 8 servings

# CHOCOLATE PIE

Mix and cook in double boiler until thick the following:

1 cup sugar
3 eggs separated
½ cup flour

2 cups milk
1 heaping tablespoon cocoa

Add and mix thoroughly:

1 teaspoon vanilla

⅓ cup butter

Stir with wire whip.

Top with meringue made from:

3 egg whites
⅓ cup sugar

1 teaspoon vanilla
1 tablespoon cornstarch

Bake at 350 degrees for 10-15 minutes.

# MEATS AND CASSEROLES

# APPLE TUNA CASSEROLE

2 cups macaroni
6 tablespoons butter or
  margarine
¼ cup all-purpose flour
3 cups milk
2 cups (8-ounces) sharp process
  American cheese, shredded

2 (6½ or 7-ounce) cans tuna,
  drained
2 cups tart apples, cored, pared
  and diced
2 tablespoons butter or
  margarine, melted
½ cup soft bread crumbs

Cook macaroni according to package directions; drain. In saucepan, melt 6 tablespoons butter or margarine over low heat. Blend in flour and ¾ teaspoon salt. Add milk all at once. Cook quickly, stirring constantly, until mixture thickens and bubbles. Add cheese; stir until cheese is melted. Stir in tuna, diced apples and drained macaroni; turn into 12x7x2-inch baking dish. Combine melted butter and crumbs. Sprinkle on top of casserole. Bake in 350 degrees oven for 30 minutes, or until apples are tender.

Yield: 8 servings

# APPLE TOPPED CHOPS

6 pork chops
1 medium onion, sliced thin
3 apples, cored and sliced
½ cup raisins
1 tablespoon brown sugar

1 teaspoon salt
¼ teaspoon nutmeg
½ teaspoon basil
⅛ teaspoon ground cloves
1 cup apple juice

Brown chops; transfer to baking dish. Cover chops with onion and apple slices. Sprinkle with raisins. Combine brown sugar and spices; sprinkle over all. Add apple juice to baking dish and cover. Bake at 350 degrees for 1 hour. Remove cover and bake an additional 30 minutes.

# APPLESAUCE MEATBALLS

2 pounds ground beef
1 cup soft bread crumbs
1 cup applesauce

2 eggs, beaten
Salt and pepper
Sauce (recipe follows)

Mix above ingredients and form into balls and chill. Roll in flour and brown in oil. Drain off excess oil and put on paper towels to drain.

Sauce:

2 cups tomato juice
1 onion, diced
1 carrot, diced

1 green pepper, diced
1 or 2 celery stalks, diced

Combine ingredients in saucepan and cook until mixture thickens. Place meatballs in casserole; pour sauce over top and cover. Bake 30 to 35 minutes at 350 degrees.

# CHICKEN LIVER-AND-APPLE BROCHETTES

½ cup cider or apple juice
3 tablespoons soy sauce
¼ teaspoon leaf thyme,
    crumbled
¼ teaspoon ground cinnamon

⅛ teaspoon ground cloves
1 cup chicken livers
1 eating apple
12 slices bacon

Mix apple cider, soy sauce, thyme, cinnamon and cloves; pour over livers in small bowl; cover and marinate in refrigerator several hours. Cut each liver in 2 or 3 pieces. Quarter and core apple; cut into bite-size chunks; halve bacon crosswise. Wrap a piece of liver and a piece of apple in each ½ slice of bacon; secure with wooden picks. Arrange on rack in broiler pan; brush with marinade. Broil 3 to 4-inches from heat for 5 minutes, turning once or twice, until bacon is crisp and livers well cooked.

Yield: about 2 dozen

# APPLE-CURRY CHICKEN

1 broiler-fryer (about 2½ to 3
　pounds), cut up
Salt and pepper to taste
¼ cup butter or margarine
2 to 3 apples, peeled and diced

½ cup minced onion
2 tablespoons curry powder
2 tablespoons flour
1½ cups chicken broth
Hot cooked rice

Sprinkle chicken with salt and pepper. In large skillet fry a few pieces at a time in butter until golden brown, removing pieces as they brown. Add apples and onion to skillet and sauté until tender. Add curry powder and flour; cook and stir 2 minutes. Blend in broth; cook and stir until thickened. Return chicken to skillet, cover and simmer 20 to 25 minutes or until tender. Serve with rice.

Yield: 4 servings

For microwave oven cook apples, onion and butter in 4-quart glass casserole 8 minutes, stirring 3 times. Stir in curry powder and flour until smooth; blend in *only 1 cup chicken broth.* Add chicken pieces seasoned with salt and pepper and spoon some of mixture over layers or equivalent.

# APPLE CASSEROLE

¾ cup margarine
2 cups sugar
2 eggs
1½ teaspoons cinnamon
1½ teaspoons soda

1 teaspoon salt
2 cups all-purpose flour
½ cup chopped pecans
3 cups hard juicy apples, diced

Cream together margarine, sugar and eggs. Sift dry ingredients together. Combine all ingredients; mix well. Bake at 350 degrees for 45 minutes.

# APPLE SMOTHERED PORK CHOPS

6 center-cut loin pork chops,
  ¾-inch thick
1 teaspoon salt
¼ teaspoon ground sage
3 tart apples

3 tablespoons molasses
3 tablespoons all-purpose flour
2 cups hot water
1 tablespoon cider vinegar
⅓ cup yellow raisins

Sprinkle pork chops with ½ teaspoon salt and ¼ teaspoon sage. Brown chops slowly in hot frying pan. Reserve fat drippings in pan. Put chops in large shallow baking dish. Peel and core apples, cut into thin slices; arrange on top of pork chops. Pour molasses on top. Stir flour into fat in frying pan; cook until brown, stirring. Gradually stir in water and cook until mixture boils. Add vinegar, ½ teaspoon salt and raisins. Pour sauce over apples and pork chops. Cover and bake in preheated 350 degrees oven for about 1 hour.

Yield: 6 servings

# DRIED APPLE-POTATO CASSEROLE

2 tablespoons margarine
1 large onion, chopped
3 cups potatoes, peeled and
  cubed

1 cup dried apples (soaked for
  2 hours and drained)
½ teaspoon salt
3 tablespoons honey (optional)

Melt margarine in covered saucepan. Add onion and sauté until it is transparent. Add the potatoes, apples, honey and salt; add about ¾ cup water. Cover and cook slowly about 30 minutes, or until the potatoes are tender. Serve with meat—either pork or beef.

# APPLE-CHEESE QUICHE

Pastry for two 9-inch pie shells
2 cups (8-ounces) sharp Cheddar
  cheese, shredded
1 pound mild sausage, cooked,
  drained and crumbled
2 cups cooking apples, peeled
  and sliced
1 can (4-ounces) mushrooms,
  sliced and drained

4 eggs
1 tablespoon all-purpose flour
1 teaspoon salt
1 cup evaporated milk
1½ tablespoons butter or
  margarine, melted
1 apple, peeled and sliced
  (optional)

Line two 9-inch quiche dishes or pie plates with pastry; trim excess
pastry around edges. Prick bottom and sides of quiche shell with a fork;
bake at 400 degrees for 8 minutes. Let cool on rack. Layer cheese,
sausage, 2 cups apples and mushrooms into pastry shells. Combine
eggs, flour, salt, milk and butter; beat well. Pour half of egg mixture into
each pastry shell. Bake at 375 degrees for 45 minutes, or until set. Top
with apple slices, if desired. Let stand 5 minutes before serving.

Yield: two 9-inch pies

# GLAZED APPLES AND FRANKS

3 tablespoons margarine
2 tablespoons prepared mustard
¾ cup light corn syrup

1 pound frankfurters
3 cups red apples, cut into 1-inch
  slices

Melt margarine in large skillet; blend in mustard and corn syrup. Slash
each frank diagonally in 3 places at 1-inch intervals. Add franks and
apples to skillet. Cover and simmer over low heat for 15 minutes.

# BAKED
# AND GLAZED
# APPLES

# BAKED APPLES WITH CURRANTS

12 apples (use large, firm
   Cortland or Rome Beauty
   apples)

Filling:
1 cup brown sugar

½ cup butter, melted
½ cup pecan nut meats
½ cup currants
12 cinnamon sticks

Slice a piece from the bottom of each apple, so it will sit firmly in the baking dish. Core each apple, being careful not to pierce through the bottom. Make a well in center of each apple (where you have removed core) large enough to hold a generous amount of the filling. Mix filling ingredients together, *except* cinnamon. Place apples in a buttered baking dish. Stuff each apple with filling. Place a cinnamon stick in center of each. Bake apples in a 300 degree oven for 30 to 35 minutes, until they are soft; yet still retain their shape.

Yield: 10 to 12 servings

# CINNAMON APPLES

6 small apples
¼ cup red cinnamon candies

2 cups sugar
2 cups water

Wash apples, pare and core. Combine sugar and cinnamon candies. Boil 5 minutes. Add apples and cook slowly until tender. Cinnamon extract and red food coloring may be substituted for cinnamon candies. If desired, apples may be cut in halves or quartered.

Yield: 6 servings

# BAKED APPLES IN WINE
*Rosé gives special flavor to a flavored fruit dessert*

4 large baking apples
¼ cup packed brown sugar
¼ teaspoon ground nutmeg

4 teaspoons butter or margarine
1 cup rosé
½ cup dairy sour cream

Core apples; pare strip from top of each. Place apples in 8x8x2-inch baking dish. Stir together brown sugar and ground nutmeg; spoon into apple centers. Top each with 1 teaspoon of the butter or margarine; pour wine into baking dish. Bake, uncovered, in 350 degrees oven for 1 hour, basting with wine occasionally. Serve warm. If desired, top each with dollop of sour cream and sprinkle with additional ground nutmeg.

Yield: 4 servings

# BOURBON APPLES

4 large crisp apples
6 tablespoons light brown sugar
Juice of ½ lemon, about 1½
    tablespoons

½ cup bourbon
4 scoops vanilla ice cream

Peel, core, and cut apples into bite-size chunks; place in a large 10-inch skillet. Add brown sugar, lemon juice, and bourbon. Cover and simmer until apples are tender, stirring occasionally and basting with liquid. Serve warm over scoops of vanilla ice cream.

Yield: 4 servings

# BAKED APPLES WITH MERINGUE

6 large baking apples                    2 egg whites
9 tablespoons sugar, divided             Custard sauce (recipe follows)
Ground cinnamon

Wash and core apples, and place in a baking pan. Fill each apple with 1 tablespoon sugar; sprinkle cinnamon on top of each. Bake apples at 350 degrees for 35 minutes. Beat egg whites until soft peaks form. Gradually add remaining 3 tablespoons sugar, 1 tablespoon at a time, continuing to beat until stiff peaks form and sugar is completely dissolved. Spoon meringue on top of each apple, and return apples to oven until meringue is lightly browned (about 10 minutes). Serve with custard sauce.

Custard Sauce:

1 egg yolk                               1 cup milk
½ cup sugar                              ½ teaspoon vanilla extract
½ teaspoon cornstarch

Combine egg yolk, sugar and cornstarch in top of a double boiler, stirring well. Gradually stir in milk. Place over boiling water; cook, stirring constantly, until mixture thickens. Remove from heat; stir in vanilla. Chill well.

Yield: 6 servings

# GLAZED APPLES

3 tablespoons butter or                  Dash of salt
   margarine                             3 tart apples, unpeeled, thinly
⅓ cup brown sugar                           sliced
½ teaspoon ground cinnamon

Melt butter in skillet. Stir in brown sugar, cinnamon and salt; add apples. Cook 10 to 15 minutes, stirring occasionally until apples are tender and glazed.

Yield: 4 servings

# SLICED APPLES IN WINE

5 large apples
1 cup red wine
6 tablespoons sugar
2 whole cloves
1 cinnamon stick

2 (2-inch) strips lemon rind
¼ cup raisins
1 teaspoon cornstarch
2 teaspoons water
1 tablespoon port wine

Peel and core apples; slice into thick slices. In a saucepan heat red wine, sugar, cloves, cinnamon stick and lemon rind. Add apple slices; cover and cook until tender. Transfer apples to a shallow 1-quart baking dish. Add raisins to sauce in saucepan; simmer 5 minutes. Combine cornstarch and water; stir into sauce. Cook until slightly thickened. Pour mixture over apples. Carefully stir in port wine. Chill.

Yield: 4 servings

# BAKED CARAMEL APPLES

4 large apples
1 tablespoon butter or margarine
1 tablespoon flour
1 cup brown sugar

1 cup boiling water
1½ cups miniature marshmallows
1 teaspoon vanilla

Peel, core and ¼ apples; place in 2-quart baking dish. Melt butter in medium saucepan; blend in flour. Add sugar and water, stirring over low heat until dissolved. Add marshmallows and continue stirring until melted. Bring sauce to boil; pour over apples. Bake at 350 degrees for 25 to 30 minutes, basting with sauce occasionally. Serve warm or cold.

Yield: 4 to 6 servings

# BAKED APPLES

6 tart apples
6 tablespoons sugar
1 tablespoon butter

½ teaspoon nutmeg
½ cup water

Select medium apples. Wash, remove stems, cores and blossom ends. Peel a narrow strip from upper part of apple. Place apples in baking dish. Combine sugar and nutmeg; spoon equally into cored apples. Dot with butter. Pour water around apples. Preheat oven to 375 degrees. Bake covered for 30 minutes, basting 2 or 3 times. Uncover, baste again and bake 15 minutes longer, or until tender.

Yield: 6 servings

VARIATION: May use honey instead of sugar, and substitute cinnamon for nutmeg.

# SAUTÉED CINNAMON APPLES

6 tablespoons butter
6 Greening or pippin apples,
  peeled, cored and sliced

2½ tablespoons vanilla sugar
  mixed with ⅛ to ¼ teaspoon
  cinnamon

Melt butter in large skillet over medium heat. Add apples, sprinkle with vanilla sugar mixture and sauté, turning carefully with spatula, until delicately browned. Serve immediately.

Yield: 8 servings

# SPECIAL
# APPLE TREATS

# CHOCOLATE DIPPED APPLES

2 cups (11½-ounce package)
  chocolate morsels
⅓ cup vegetable shortening
8 to 10 medium size apples

Coconut (optional)
Chopped nuts (optional)
Wooden sticks (optional)

Melt over hot (not boiling) water, milk chocolate morsels and vegetable shortening. Remove from heat. Insert wooden sticks in apples if desired. Dip apples, one at a time, into chocolate mixture, using stick or a large spoon or rubber spatula. Apple should be completely coated with chocolate mixture. Garnish with coconut or nuts, if desired. Place on waxed paper-lined cookie sheets. Chill until chocolate coating sets. Serve immediately or keep in refrigerator until ready to serve.

Yield: 8 to 10 servings

# CARAMEL APPLE WITCHES

49 (14-ounce bag) caramels
2 tablespoons water
4 or 5 medium apples

Wooden sticks
Miniature marshmallows
Candy corn

Melt caramels with water in 1½ quart saucepan over low heat, stirring until sauce is smooth. Wash and dry apples; insert stick into stem end of each apple. Dip into hot caramel sauce; turn until coated. Scrape off sauce from bottom of apples. Place on greased waxed paper. Create eyes and mouth with miniature marshmallow halves. Create nose with candy corn. Make hat from construction paper, leaving opening for wooden stick.

Yield: 4 to 5 servings

# PEANUT BUTTER APPLES

8 wooden skewers
8 medium-size apples, stems
  removed
2 cups (12-ounce package) peanut
  butter chips

3 tablespoons vegetable oil
Chopped nuts, crushed cereals
  or coconut (optional)

Wash apples and dry thoroughly, insert wooden skewer into each. Set aside. In heavy 1½ quart saucepan, melt peanut butter chips with oil over very low heat; stir constantly until smooth. Remove from heat. Working quickly, dip apples in peanut butter mixture and twirl to remove excess coating. Roll in chopped nuts, crushed cereal or coconut, if desired. Allow to cool on buttered or waxed paper-covered cookie sheet. Refrigerate if desired.

Yield: 8 servings

# APPLE CARTWHEELS

8 medium apples
1 cup (6-ounce package) semi-
  sweet chocolate morsels

½ cup peanut butter
¼ cup raisins
1 tablespoon honey

Remove core from each apple, leaving a cavity 1¼-inches in diameter. Set aside. In blender container, process semi-sweet chocolate morsels 5 seconds or until morsels are chopped. In a small bowl, mix chopped chocolate, peanut butter, raisins and honey. Stuff cored apples with chocolate-peanut butter filling. Wrap each apple with plastic wrap. Chill in refrigerator. When ready to serve, slice crosswise in ½-inch slices.

Yield: 32 cartwheels

# BROILED APPLE AND CHEESE SANDWICH

6 slices toast (crusts trimmed)        6 apples, unpeeled, sliced
Mayonnaise                             Margarine (melted)
Sliced Cheese                          12 slices partially broiled bacon
Brown Sugar

For each sandwich spread a slice of toast with mayonnaise. Cover with a slice of cheese and an apple slice which has been brushed with melted margarine, sprinkle lightly with brown sugar and broil. Top with two slices of partially broiled bacon and place the sandwich under low broiler heat in a moderate oven 350 degrees until cheese is melted and the bacon is crisp. Serve hot.

Yield: 6 servings

# APPLE SANDWICHES

2 apples, finely chopped          ½ cup mayonnaise
¼ cup raisins                     2 teaspoons lemon juice
6 to 8-ounces cooked ham,         12 slices hot buttered toast
    finely diced                  6 lettuce leaves
¼ cup (1-ounce) shredded
    mild Cheddar cheese

Combine apples, raisins, ham, cheese, mayonnaise, and lemon juice; mix well. Spread about ½ cup apple mixture on each of 6 slices of toast. Top with lettuce leaves and remaining toast. Cut sandwiches in half, and serve immediately.

Yield: 6 servings

# HOT APPLE SOUP

1 tablespoon butter
1 large onion, chopped
4 cups (1 quart) chicken stock
2 large green apples, cored,
  peeled and chopped
¾ teaspoon curry powder, or to
  taste

Juice of ½ large lemon
3 tablespoons butter
¼ cup all-purpose flour
½ cup half and half

Melt 1 tablespoon butter in a large saucepan over medium-high heat. Add onion and sauté until soft but not brown. Stir in stock, apples, curry powder and lemon juice and bring to boil. Reduce heat and let simmer for about 10 minutes. Melt remaining butter in another large saucepan over medium heat until foam subsides. Blend in flour and cook 1 to 2 minutes, stirring constantly. Gradually stir in soup until well blended. When mixture reaches boiling point, remove from heat.

Yield: 6 to 8 servings

# APPLE-HERB STUFFING

1½ cups onion, chopped
½ cup celery, sliced
6 tablespoons butter or
  margarine
3 cups apples, finely diced and
  cored
3 cups whole-wheat bread cubes

¼ cup parsley, chopped
½ teaspoon leaf sage, crumbled
½ teaspoon leaf thyme, crumbled
¼ teaspoon ground nutmeg
2 envelopes or teaspoons instant
  chicken broth
½ cup hot water

Sauté onion and celery in butter in skillet until soft, 5 minutes. Stir in apples; continue cooking and stirring 3 to 5 minutes. Remove from heat. Combine with bread, parsley, sage, thyme, nutmeg, instant chicken broth and water. Toss until evenly moist.

This stuffing is versatile—it is also good with roast chicken, baked ham slices or braised sausages.

Yield: about 5 cups

# HONEY APPLE RINGS
*Excellent as a garnish*

½ cup honey
2 tablespoons vinegar
¼ teaspoon salt
¼ teaspoon ground cinnamon

4 medium cooking apples,
unpeeled, cored, and cut into
½-inch rings

Combine honey, vinegar, salt, and cinnamon in a large skillet; bring to a boil. Add apple rings; reduce heat and simmer 8 to 10 minutes, turning apples once.

Yield: 8 servings

# RED APPLE RELISH

4½ cups tart red apples, finely
chopped
½ cup water
¼ cup lemon juice
½ cup raisins

1 package powdered pectin
5½ cups sugar
½ cup nuts, chopped
Red food coloring (optional)

Wash, core but do not pare apples. Chop apples fine. Combine apples, lemon juice and raisins in kettle. Add pectin and stir well. Bring to a full boil over entire surface. Add sugar and continue stirring; heat again to full bubbling boil. Boil hard 1 minute, stirring constantly. Add the nuts; remove from heat. If desired, add 3 to 4 drops of red food coloring. Skim the relish, ladle into hot containers, and seal immediately.

Yield: seven ½ pints

# APPLE RELISH

14 large apples
2 red sweet peppers

2 green sweet peppers
8 onions

Prepare and chop in small cubes, add 2 cups brown sugar and mix together. Cover with vinegar in cooking kettle, boil 20 minutes. Pack in sterilized jars and seal.

*Mrs. Eunice Ogle*
*Gatlinburg, Tennessee*

# BUTTERS, JELLIES AND SAUCES

# APPLE BUTTER

1 peck tart apples, unpeeled
4 cups water
10 cups sugar (about)

2 teaspoons ground cloves
2 tablespoons ground cinnamon
1 teaspoon ground allspice

Wash, quarter and cook apples with water. Cover; let simmer slowly until tender. Rub through coarse sieve. Should be about 5 quarts of pulp. Add ½ as much sugar as pulp; add spices. Simmer about 2 hours, stirring frequently as it will scorch easily. An asbestos mat placed under kettle will prevent scorching. When thickened, pour into hot sterilized jars; seal immediately. Apple butter becomes stiffer when cool. Delicious served on hot buttered toast.

Yield: 9 to 10 pints

# SPICY APPLE BUTTER

4 large apples, peeled, cored and
   sliced
1 cup apple cider

½ cup brown sugar
¼ cup hard red cinnamon candies

In a 2-quart pan, cook sliced apples and cider over medium heat, stirring occasionally, until apples reach the consistency of applesauce. Remove mixture from heat and push through a fine colander before returning to pan and adding brown sugar and cinnamon candies. Continue cooking over medium heat, stirring often, until very thick. When a bit is dropped on a glass plate and it holds its shape, the apple butter is done. Pour cooled apple butter into a glass container and refrigerate.

Yield: 2 cups

# CIDER APPLE BUTTER

8 pounds apples
4 quarts sweet cider
3 pounds sugar

1 teaspoon cloves
1 teaspoon cinnamon

The apples are pared, cored and sliced. Cook slowly in the cider. When this is cooked enough, sugar is slowly added, along with the spices. Keep cooking and stirring the sauce until the mixture is no longer watery but thick. Good apple butter should be a dark color and be thick enough to cling to a knife.

# CINNAMON APPLE JELLY

3 pounds tart apples
3 cups sugar

1 drop oil of cinnamon
6 drops red food coloring

Wash fruit; do not pare or core. Cut into eighths, removing blemishes. Barely cover with water; simmer until soft. Strain juice through jelly bag. Measure 4 cups juice into large kettle. Add sugar; stir until dissolved. Bring to full rolling boil over high heat. Boil hard until syrup sheets off spoon, about 8 degrees above the boiling point of water. Remove from heat; skim off foam quickly. Add cinnamon and coloring. Pour into hot scalded glasses. Seal immediately with paraffin.

Yield: 4 half-pint glasses

# APPLE-CRANBERRY CONSERVE

5 apples, unpeeled, cored and
    ground
3 cups fresh cranberries, ground
1 orange, unpeeled, seeded
    and ground
1 lemon, unpeeled, seeded and
    ground

1 (20-ounce) can crushed
    pineapple, undrained
1 (1¾-ounce) package powdered
    fruit pectin
5½ cups sugar
1 (2¼-ounce) package slivered
    almonds, toasted

Combine fruit in a large Dutch oven; stir well. Place over high heat and bring to a boil, stirring frequently. Stir in fruit pectin, and return to a boil, and boil 1 minute, stirring frequently. Stir in fruit pectin, and return to a boil and boil 1 minute, stirring constantly. Remove from heat, and skim off foam with a metal spoon. Stir in almonds. Quickly spoon conserve into hot sterilized jars, leaving ¼ inch head space; cover at once with metal lids, and screw bands tight. Process in boiling water bath 5 minutes.

Yield: 11 half-pints

# APPLE-PEACH CONSERVE

2 cups tart apples, chopped
    and pared
2 cups peaches, peeled and
    chopped

⅓ cup lemon juice
3 cups sugar

Combine all ingredients. Cook slowly for 20 minutes. Pour into hot scalded jars; seal at once.

Yield: 4 half-pints

# APPLE MARMALADE

8 cups apples, peeled and
  sliced
7 cups sugar
1 tablespoon cinnamon
1 teaspoon cloves

¼ teaspoon nutmeg
¼ teaspoon salt
4 tablespoons lemon juice
2 cups cider

Mix ingredients; cook slowly. Stir frequently until mixture thickens. It
will take an hour of slow cooking. Pour into sterilized jars and seal immediately.

# MINT-APPLE JELLY

4 cups canned apple juice
1 (2½-ounce) package powdered
  fruit pectin
6 drops green food coloring

1 cup fresh mint leaves, lightly
  packed
4½ cups sugar

Combine apple juice, pectin, food coloring and mint leaves in very large
kettle. Bring to hard boil. Stir in sugar. Again bring to rolling boil; boil
hard 2 minutes, stirring constantly. Remove from heat; remove leaves.
Pour into hot scalded jars; seal.

Yield: 6 half-pint jars

# CIDER BAKED APPLESAUCE

12 tart apples, peeled, cored
   and sliced
2 lemon rinds
½ cup apple cider

1 cinnamon stick, broken
   into pieces
4 tablespoons butter
¼ cup brown sugar

Place apples and cinnamon stick in casserole. Sprinkle with lemon rind. Pour cider over all; bring to boil on top of stove. Cover and place in 350 degrees oven. Bake for 30 minutes. Remove from oven and discard cinnamon stick. Put apples through food mill or coarse sieve. Add butter and sugar. Serve warm with a spoonful of sour cream.

Yield: 8 servings

# CHUNKY STYLE APPLESAUCE

8 large apples, peeled, cored
   and cut into thick slices
⅛ cup water
½ cup sugar

⅛ teaspoon allspice
⅛ teaspoon cloves
¼ teaspoon cinnamon

Combine apples, water and sugar into saucepan. Bring to boil. Watch very carefully and simmer 4 minutes or until apples are part sauce and part whole. *Do not over cook.* It should be thick. Turn off heat and add spices as indicated or to taste. Excellent with roast pork, duck or potato pancakes. Freezes very well!

Yield: 6 servings

# BEVERAGES

# HOT CIDER PUNCH

2 cups water
1 tablespoon ginger
1 tablespoon nutmeg
6 whole cloves
6 whole allspice

2 (2-inch) cinnamon sticks
1 gallon apple cider
2 cups sugar
1½ cups brown sugar, firmly
   packed

Combine water and spices in large saucepan; cover and bring to a boil. Boil 10 minutes. Add apple cider and sugar. Simmer over low heat 10 minutes, stirring frequently. Serve hot.

Yield: 5 quarts

*Mrs. Margaret S. Love*
*5565 Shelby Oaks Drive*
*Memphis, Tennessee 38134*

# HOT BUTTERED RUM CIDER

1 quart apple cider
2 tablespoons sugar
2 teaspoons butter

2 teaspoons rum flavoring
Nutmeg

Combine apple cider, sugar and butter; bring to boil. Remove from heat and add flavoring. Pour into mugs and sprinkle with nutmeg.

Yield: 4 to 6 servings

# HOT CIDER

6 cups cider
1 to 2 sticks cinnamon

½ teaspoon whole cloves

Heat in saucepan to simmer or perk in coffee pot with spices in coffee pot basket.

*Variations:*
Add a twist of lemon, or add 1 (6 ounce) can frozen lemonade concentrate, or eliminate spices and add ⅛ cup red cinnamon candies.

# APPLE BLOSSOMS

1 quart chilled apple cider
2 cups chilled pink dinner wine
2 tablespoons lemon juice

½ cup extra fine sugar
Club Soda
Ice

Combine apple cider, wine, lemon juice and sugar; stir until sugar is dissolved. Pour over ice in tall glasses filling ¾ full. Fill to top with Club Soda.

Yield: 6 to 8 servings

# SODA-FOUNTAIN CIDER

1½ cups sugar
2 cups water
1 quart sweet cider

1 pint orange juice
½ cup lemon juice

Cook sugar and water for a few minutes. Pour in cider, orange juice and lemon juice. When it cools, strain. Place into freezer until it becomes partly ice, and serve.

# FROSTY APPLE SHAKE

1 quart apple cider (chilled)
1 pint vanilla ice cream
  (softened)
1 (8¾-ounce) can crushed
  pineapple (optional)

½ teaspoon cinnamon
Nutmeg (optional)

Combine in blender or mixer the apple cider, ice cream, crushed pine-apple and cinnamon; mix until frothy. Sprinkle with nutmeg.

# QUICK CIDER PUNCH

1 tray cider ice cubes, frozen
2 quarts sweet cider

Mint leaves, fresh

Freeze 1 tray of ice cubes using sweet cider instead of water. Place 1 ice cube in each highball glass. Fill with cold cider and top off with fresh mint leaves.

# RED APPLE CIDER

1 quart hard cider
2 tablespoons grenadine
6 whole cloves

¼ teaspoon ground nutmeg
Dark rum
Cinnamon sticks

Combine cider, grenadine, cloves and nutmeg in a medium saucepan. Heat mixture until hot (do not boil). Ladle into mugs; add about 1 tablespoon rum to each. Garnish each serving with a cinnamon stick.

# CHAMPAGNE MOCKTAIL

1 cup chilled apple juice
1 cup chilled ginger ale

Thin lemon slices

Just before serving, combine apple juice and ginger ale. Serve in stemmed glasses with a lemon slice in each.

Yield: 4 servings

# HOLIDAY ALE

1 quart chilled apple juice
2 cups chilled cranberry juice

2 cups chilled lemon soda

In a large pitcher, combine the apple juice, cranberry juice and lemon soda. Mix these ingredients together until the flavors are well blended; pour over ice cubes in tall glasses. Garnish with a sprig of mint or a lemon slice.

# NANCY'S ELIXIR

1 cup cold milk
1 cup apple sauce
¼ cup sugar

1 teaspoon vanilla
6 ice cubes

Place all ingredients in blender. Blend at low speed for 10 seconds, then at high speed for 10 seconds. Serve immediately.

*Variation:*
1 cup apple juice, plus ¼ cup instant nonfat dry milk may be substituted for the 1 cup milk.

Yield: 3 cups

94

## • Additional Copies •

**THE APPLE BARN COOKBOOK**

Softcover    90 pgs.

230 Apple Valley Road
Sevierville, TN 37862

Please send me_____copies of **THE APPLE BARN COOKBOOK** at $9.95 per copy, plus $3.00 per copy for postage and handling. Checks payable to Apple Barn.

Name_____

Address_____

City_____ State_____ Zip_____

## • Additional Copies •

**THE APPLE BARN COOKBOOK**

Softcover    90 pgs.

230 Apple Valley Road
Sevierville, TN 37862

Please send me_____copies of **THE APPLE BARN COOKBOOK** at $9.95 per copy, plus $3.00 per copy for postage and handling. Checks payable to Apple Barn.

Name_____

Address_____

City_____ State_____ Zip_____

## ☐ YES!  Please send me a copy of the Apple Barn Catalog.

Name_____

Address_____

City_____ State_____ Zip_____

**800-421-4606        www.AppleBarnCiderMill.com**

**ORDER FORM**